The 1920's

Teachers Guide

A Supplemental Teaching Unit
from the Records of the National Archives

NATIONAL
ARCHIVES

National Archives Trust Fund Board
National Archives and Records Administration

A B C ⬣ C L I O

ABC – CLIO, Inc
130 Cremona Drive, P.O. Box 1911
Santa Barbara, CA 93116-1911
ISBN 1-57607-785-3

Other Units in this Series:

Table of Contents

Foreword

In an effort to make the historical records in the National Archives available to an increasing number of students across the nation, the Office of Public Programs and Exhibits began in 1970 a program designed to introduce these vast resources to secondary school students. School classes visiting the National Archives were given the opportunity to work with archival materials as historians use them, by examining and interpreting original sources. Teachers and students responded enthusiastically and encouraged the development of a series of supplementary printed teaching units. This unit, *The 1920's*, is the fifth in the series. We hope that these materials will bring you and your students closer to the pleasures and the perils of working with primary sources and will enhance your instructional program.

ROBERT M. WARNER
Archivist of the United States
1981

...to bring you and your students the excitement and satisfaction of working with primary sources and to enhance your instructional program.

$\mathcal{P}$reface

◆ This unit is made up of 24 exercises.

◆ Each exercise includes reproductions of documents from the National Archives and suggests classroom activities based on these documents.

The 1920's is a teaching unit designed to supplement your students' study of the 1919-1929 decade. The unit is made up of 24 exercises that together form a mosaic of American life during those years. Each exercise includes reproductions of documents from the National Archives and suggests classroom activities based on these documents. The documents include personal letters, news clippings, photographs, graphs, maps, and telegrams. Students practice the historian's skills as they complete exercises using these documents to gather information, identify points of view, weigh evidence, form hypotheses, and draw conclusions.

The documents in this unit do not reflect every topic usually included in a history textbook. In some instances, the federal government had no interest in or authority over a given event and therefore compiled no records on it. In other cases, documents in the National Archives on several historical topics proved to be limited (Sacco and Vanzetti) or difficult to use in the classroom (Teapot Dome Scandal). However, the documents included here do reflect a wide range of social, political, economic, and cultural themes of the decade as seen from the points of view of citizens who corresponded with the federal government.

The 1920's was a period of heightened racial tension and ethnocentrism. Within this unit are documents that reflect these attitudes. These documents are typical of hundreds within the files of the National Archives. They were selected, as were all the documents within this unit, as reflections of the time being studied, not as a means of perpetuating these attitudes. As you use these documents in your classroom, we encourage you to help students analyze them objectively.

National Archives education specialist Mary Alexander and director of public programs Elsie Freeman Finch developed this publication. We are pleased to issue a revised and updated set of these documentary teaching materials.

WYNELL B. SCHAMEL
LEE ANN POTTER
Education Specialists
2001

The 1920's is a teaching unit designed to supplement your students' study of the 1919-1929 decade.

Acknowledgments

Many people helped in the original production of this unit. They included National Archives staff members Bruce Ashkenas, Stanley Brown, Ronald Grim, William Grover, Douglas Helms, Jerry Hess, Joseph Howerton, David Kepley, Bill Leary, Lane Moore, Donald Mosholder, Fred Pernell, Leonard Rapport, John Roberts, Edward Schamel, John Vernon, and Richard Wood.

Special thanks go to Virginia Cardwell Purdy, Director of the National Archives Education Division, whose imagination sparked the project. As it developed, the advice, criticism, and encouragement of Charles L. Mitsakos, Andover, MA, Public Schools, was invaluable.

Teachers and social studies administrators in workshops and programs here and across the country reviewed the unit. Their reactions and comments shaped and improved it. As colleagues in this endeavor, their suggestions were invaluable.

Others whose advice and constructive criticism moved the project along include David Fell, Lillian Grandy, Nancy Malan, Debra Newman, Leslie Rowland, and John Rumbarger. Kathryn Gent, a student at Moravian College, prepared the bibliography and time line. Robb Storm, from the staff of the Nixon Presidential Library, reviewed the unit for historical content. Vonda Yunker, a social studies teacher at Northern High School in Garrett County, MD, reviewed the unit for its educational validity and usefulness.

During the republication process, we were ably assisted by George Mason University intern Adam Jevec; volunteers Elizabeth S. Lourie, Jane Douma Pearson, and Donald Alderson; and National Archives staff members Michael Hussey, A.J. Daverede, Patrick Osborn, Amy Patterson, Kate Flaherty, Donald Roe, and Charles Mayn.

Publisher's Note

Primary source documents have long been a cornerstone of ABC-CLIO's commitment to producing high-quality, learner-centered history and social studies resources. When our nation's students have the opportunity to interact with the undiluted artifacts of the past, they can better understand the breadth of the human experience and the present state of affairs.

It is with great enthusiasm that we celebrate the release of this series of teaching units designed in partnership with the National Archives—materials that we hope will bring historical context and deeper knowledge to U.S. middle and high school students. Each unit has been revised and updated, including new bibliographic references. Each teaching unit has been correlated to the curriculum standards for the teaching of social studies and history developed by the National Council for the Social Studies and the National Center for History in the Schools.

For more effective use of these teaching units in the classroom, each booklet is accompanied by an interactive CD-ROM which includes exercise worksheets, digital images of original documents, and, for four titles, sound recordings. A videocassette of motion pictures accompanies the teaching unit *The United States At War: 1944*. For those who would like to order facsimiles of primary source documents in their original sizes, or additional titles in this series, we have included an order form to make it easy for you to do so.

The mission of the National Archives is "to ensure ready access to the essential evidence that documents the rights of American citizens, the actions of Federal officials, and the national experience."

These units go a long way toward fulfilling that mission, helping the next generation of American citizens develop a clear understanding of the nation's past and a firm grasp of the role of the individual in guiding the nation's future. ABC-CLIO is honored to be part of this process.

BECKY SNYDER
Publisher & Vice President
ABC-CLIO Schools

> The mission of the National Archives is "to ensure ready access to the essential evidence that documents the rights of American citizens, the actions of Federal officials, and the national experience."

Teaching With Documents Curriculum Standards Correlations

The National Council for the Social Studies and the National Center for History in the Schools have developed a set of comprehensive curriculum standards for the teaching of social studies and history. Take a look at how thoroughly the Teaching With Documents series supports the curriculum.

National Council for the Social Studies / National Center for History in the Schools

Document	CULTURE	TIME, CONTINUITY & CHANGE	PEOPLE, PLACES & ENVIRONMENT	INDIVIDUAL DEVELOPMENT & IDENTITY	INDIVIDUALS, GROUPS & INSTITUTIONS	POWER, AUTHORITY & GOVERNANCE	PRODUCTION, DISTRIBUTION & CONSUMPTION	SCIENCE, TECHNOLOGY & SOCIETY	GLOBAL CONNECTIONS	CIVIC IDEALS & PRACTICES	CHRONOLOGICAL THINKING	HISTORICAL COMPREHENSION	HISTORICAL ANALYSIS & INTERPRETATION	HISTORICAL RESEARCH CAPABILITIES	HISTORICAL ISSUES-ANALYSIS & DECISION-MAKING
The Constitution: Evolution of a Government	●	●	●	●	●	●	●		●	●	●	●	●	●	
The Bill of Rights: Evolution of Personal Liberties		●	●	●	●	●				●	●	●	●	●	
The United States Expands West: 1785–1842	●	●	●	●	●	●		●	●		●	●	●	●	
Westward Expansion: 1842–1912	●		●	●	●	●	●				●	●	●	●	
The Civil War: Soldiers and Civilians			●	●	●	●					●	●	●	●	
The Progressive Years: 1898–1917		●	●		●	●		●	●		●	●	●	●	
World War I: The Home Front		●		●		●					●	●	●	●	
The 1920's		●	●	●	●	●		●		●	●	●	●	●	
The Great Depression and The New Deal World		●	●	●	●		●				●	●	●	●	●
War II: The Home Front	●	●									●	●	●	●	●
The United States At War: 1944		●			●			●		●	●	●	●	●	●
The Truman Years: 1945–1953					●	●	●	●	●		●	●	●	●	●
Peace and Prosperity: 1953–1961	●			●	●	●		●	●		●	●	●	●	●

National Council for the Social Studies

CULTURE—should provide for the study of culture and cultural diversity

TIME, CONTINUITY & CHANGE—should provide for the study of the ways people view themselves in and over time

PEOPLE, PLACES & ENVIRONMENT—should provide for study of people, places, and environments

INDIVIDUAL DEVELOPMENT & IDENTITY—should provide for the study of individual development and identity

INDIVIDUALS, GROUPS & INSTITUTIONS—should provide for the study of interactions among individuals, groups, and institutions

POWER, AUTHORITY & GOVERNANCE—should provide for the study of how structures of power are created and changed

PRODUCTION, DISTRIBUTION & CONSUMPTION—should provide for the study of the usage of goods and services

SCIENCE, TECHNOLOGY & SOCIETY—should provide for the study of relationships among science, technology, and society

GLOBAL CONNECTIONS—should provide for the study of global connections and interdependence

CIVIC IDEALS & PRACTICES—should provide for the study of the ideals, principles, and practices of citizenship

National Center for History in the Schools

CHRONOLOGICAL THINKING

HISTORICAL COMPREHENSION

HISTORICAL ANALYSIS & INTERPRETATION

HISTORICAL RESEARCH CAPABILITIES

HISTORICAL ISSUES-ANALYSIS & DECISION-MAKING

Introduction

This unit contains two elements: 1) a book, which contains a teachers guide and a set of reproductions of print documents, and 2) a CD-ROM, which contains the exercise worksheets from the teachers guide and a set of reproductions of documents in electronic format. In selecting the documents, we applied three standards. First, the documents must be entirely from the holdings of the National Archives and must reflect the actions of the federal government or citizens' responses to those actions. Second, each document must be typical of the hundreds of records of its kind relating to its particular topic; we have been careful not to choose exceptional or unrepresentative documents. Third, the documents must be legible and may be useful for vocabulary development. In selecting documents, we tried to choose those having appeal for young people.

Objectives

We have provided an outline of the general objectives for the unit. You will be able to achieve these objectives by completing several if not all of the exercises in the unit. Because each exercise aims to develop skills defined in the general objectives, you may be selective and still develop those skills. In addition, each exercise has its own specific objectives.

UNIT CONTAINS:

◆ **1)** a book, which contains a teachers guide and a set of reproductions of print documents, and

◆ **2)** a CD-ROM, which contains the exercise worksheets from the teachers guide and a set of reproductions of documents in electronic format.

Outline

This unit on the 1920's includes 24 exercises. Topics presented cover issues related to society at large and women, youth, and ethnic minorities in particular; changes in lifestyles, morals, technology, working conditions, and transportation; and a summary exercise designed to synthesize information from all the documents included in this unit.

List of Documents

The list of documents gives specific information (e.g., date and name of author) and record group number for each document. Records in the National Archives are arranged in record groups. A typical record group (RG) consists of the records created or accumulated by a department, agency, bureau, or other administrative unit of the federal government. Each record group is identified for retrieval purposes by a record group number; for example, RG 59 (Department of State) or RG 28 (U.S. Postal Service). Complete archival citations of all documents are listed in the appendix, page 79.

Exercise Summary Chart

The chart shows the organization of exercises 1-24. For each exercise, the chart outlines the materials needed, the document content, the student activities that are emphasized, and the number of class periods needed. Review the chart carefully and decide which exercises to use based on your objectives for the students, their ability levels, and the content you wish to teach. The exercises may be adapted to fit your objectives and teaching style.

Introductory Exercises

Before starting exercises 1-24, it is important to familiarize students with documents and their importance to the historian who interprets them and writes history from them. We suggest that you direct students to do one or both of the introductory exercises, which are generic and can be used with most documents, wherever they are found. The Written Document Analysis, p. 12, is designed to help students analyze systematically any written document in the unit. The Historian's Tools, p. 13, is designed to increase student awareness of the process of analyzing historical information and is most appropriate for students working at or above 9th grade reading level. The Cartoon Analysis, p. 15, can be used to analyze systematically political cartoons.

Classroom Exercises

This unit contains two dozen suggested exercises on 1920's topics. Within the explanatory material for each of the exercises, you will find the following information:

- ➤ Note to the teacher
- ➤ Classroom time required
- ➤ Objectives (specific)
- ➤ Materials needed
- ➤ Procedures
- ➤ Student worksheets

You may choose to combine several exercises on a topic within the unit. For example, exercises 7, 11, 12, and 13 address the problems and concerns of blacks in the 1920's. In some instances a document is used in more than one exercise when it is appropriate to the skill or content objectives of several exercises. We encourage you to select and adapt the exercises and documents that best suit your own teaching style.

Ability Levels

As in our other units, we developed exercises for students of different abilities. For some topics, we designed two exercises tailored to different student needs; for example, exercises 19 and 20 about prohibition. Throughout the unit we have made an effort to provide exercises in which students utilize a variety of skills, including reading for understanding, interpreting maps and graphs, and analyzing photographs and cartoons. All lessons have procedures for ability levels one, two, and three. Procedures begin with strategies designed for level three students, continue with level two strategies, and conclude with level one strategies. Our definition of each ability level is as follows:

Level One: Good reading skills, minimal direction needed from teacher to organize and interpret information from several sources, and ability to independently complete assignments;

Level Two: Average reading skills, general direction needed from teacher to organize and interpret information from several sources, and ability to complete assignments with some assistance from teacher;

Level Three: Limited reading skills, step-by-step direction needed from teacher to organize and interpret information from several sources, and ability to complete assignments with close supervision from teacher.

These ability levels are merely guides; we recognize that you will adapt the exercises to suit your students' needs and your own teaching style.

Time Line

A time line is included for use by your students. You may want to reproduce it for each student or display it.

Bibliography

As students work with the 1920's documents, they should be assigned appropriate readings from their text and other secondary sources. They should also be encouraged to use the resources of school and public libraries. To guide them, an annotated bibliography appears at the end of the Teachers Guide.

General Objectives

Upon successfully completing the exercises in this unit, students should be able to demonstrate the following skills using a single document:

➤ Identify factual evidence

➤ Identify points of view (bias and/or prejudice)

➤ Collect, reorder, and weigh the significance of evidence

➤ Develop defensible inferences, conclusions, and generalizations from factual information

Using several documents from this unit, students should be able to:

➤ Analyze the documents to compare and contrast evidence

➤ Evaluate and interpret evidence drawn from the documents

Outline of Classroom Exercises

The 1920s

List of Documents

Following the identifying information for each document reproduced in the unit, we have given the record group (RG) number in which the original can be found. Should you want copies of these documents or wish to refer to them in correspondence with us, give the complete archival citation, which is found in the appendix on page 79. **You may duplicate any of the documents in this unit for use with your students.**

Documents in *The 1920's* are taken from the following record groups: Bureau of the Census (RG 29), Children's Bureau (RG 102), Department of Justice (RG 60), Department of Labor (RG 174), Department of State (RG 59), Federal Extension Service (RG 33), Federal Mediation and Conciliation Service (RG 280), Federal Trade Commission (RG 122), International Communication Agency (RG 306), National Commission on Law Observance and Enforcement (RG 10), Office of the Secretary of Agriculture (RG 16), Public Health Service (RG 90), U.S. Coal Commission (RG 68), U.S. House of Representatives (RG 233), U.S. Postal Service (RG 28), U.S. Railroad Administration (RG 14), U.S. Senate (RG 46), and Women's Bureau (RG 86).

1. Maxwell Car Ad, *The Literary Digest*, April 11, 1925 (RG 60).

2. Cartoon, Chicago *Daily Tribune*, August 23, 1924 (RG 60). Copyrighted ©, Chicago *Tribune*. Used with permission.

3. "Girl, Boy, Bottle...," Elizabethton *Star* (TN), April 18, 1929 (RG 280).

4. Report of metropolitan police department, *17ᵗʰ Annual Reports of Departments*, 1922, Vincennes, IN (RG 68).

5. Photograph from Hood River County, OR, July 20, 1925 (RG 33).

6. Letter to Mr. [George W.] Wichersham, July 22, 1929 (RG 10).

7. Telegram from John R. Shillady, Secretary, NAACP, to Thomas R. Marshall, June 26, 1919 (RG 46).

8. Graph of trend of prices and purchasing power, n.d. (RG 16).

9. Letter to the Hon. Philander C. Knox from R. A. Craford, U.M.W. District 2, December 9, 1920 (RG 46).

10. Letter to Mr. [Henry A.] Wallace from Albert O. Fisher, August 15, 1923 (RG 16).

11. Editorial, *Wall Street Journal*, September 27, 1921 (RG 16). Reprinted by permission of the *Wall Street Journal* © Dow Jones & Company, Inc., 1921. All Rights Reserved.

12. Letter to Mr. Bradford Knapp from T. O. Walton, December 31, 1918 (RG 16).

13. "Says the Foreigner is not Appreciated," Brooklyn *Standard Union*, March 23, 1921 (RG 90).

14. Letter to the Hon. Secretary of Labor, Washington, DC, from F. A. Canizares, September 20, 1922 (RG 174).

15. Letter to U.S. Senate from Loggia Beatrice Cenci No. 1207, February 9, 1924 (RG 46).

16. Letter to President Calvin Coolidge from Alliance Klan #1, May 15, 1924 (RG 174).

17. Photograph, "Ellis Island, NY," 1923 (RG 90).

18. Letter to the Hon. Woodrow Wilson from George A. Murray, February 14, 1920 (RG 14).

19. Letter to the Hon. Henry C. Wallace from H. L. Remmel, October 3, 1923 (RG 16).

20. Letter to the Hon. Third Assistant, Division of Classification [U.S. Post Office Department], from H. C. Blalock, July 17, 1919 (RG 28).

21. Memorandum for Mr. [Walker D.] Hines from Max Thelen, June 21, 1919 (RG 14).

22. Ad, The Chicago *Defender*, September 27, 1919 (RG 28).

23. Flyer from the NAACP, n.d. (RG 46).

24. Letter to the Department of Justice from Mrs. H. Lipsett, April 19, 1929 (RG 60).

25. Letter to Walker D. Hines from M. W. Briggs, September 19, 1919 (RG 14).

26. Letter to Warren G. Harding from Ara Lee Settle, June 18, 1922 (RG 60).

27. Letter to Mrs. Mable Walker Willebrandt from Gladys W. Center, November 21, 1928 (RG 60).

28. Letter to Mr. Herbert Hoover, President, from Horace Robinson, November 20, 1929 (RG 60).

29. Survey of Pathfinders of America, ca. 1924 (RG 102).

30. Letter to the Hon. Calvin Coolidge from Charles D. Levy, June 24, 1924 (RG 60).

31. Flyer, "The Ku Klux Klan Invites You to the Portals . . .," n.d. (RG 60).

32. Letter to Warren G. Harding from Arthur James Mann, September 24, 1921 (RG 60).

33. Photograph, "KKK women marching," Washington, DC, 1928 (RG 306).

34. Letter to Attorney General [John G.] Sargeant from Rampy J. Burdick, March 3, 1928 (RG 60).

35. Photograph, "President Calvin Coolidge," n.d. (RG 306).

36. Letter to Hon. Calvin Coolidge from W. E. Ryan, July 28, 1924 (RG 60).

37. Letter to Department of Justice from Isaac McClellan, February 10, 1923 (RG 60).

38. Letter to U.S. District Attorney [Harlan F.] Stone from S. Jonce, December 5, 1924 (RG 60).

39. Photograph, "Charles A. Lindbergh loading cargo," Lambert Field, St. Louis, 1925 (RG 28).

40. Post Office Department map of airmail routes, April 24, 1926 (RG 28).

41. Post Office Department map of airmail routes, August 1, 1928 (RG 28).

42. Advertisement for laundry supplies, Montgomery Ward catalog, 1922-23 (RG 122).

43. Advertisement for the 1900 Cataract Washer, n.d. (RG 122).

44. Advertisement from Danciger Brumalt Co., n.d. (RG 60).

45. Letter to Hon. George P. McLean from Legislative Committee, Connecticut Council of Catholic Women, February 4, 1924 (RG 46).

46. House Joint Resolution 75, 68th Congress, 1st session, December 13, 1923 (RG 233).

47. Charts relating to the employment of men and women, *Statistical Atlas of the United States*, 1924, p. 256 and 267 (RG 29).

48. Photograph, "Telephone operators," April 7, 1927 (RG 86).

49. Suggested window display from *Help for the Dealer*, Landers, Frary and Clark, New Britain, CT, n.d. (RG 122).

50. Letter to the Hon. James A. Davis from J. O. Wells, April 20, 1923 (RG 174).

51. Newspaper page, the Omaha *World Herald*, November 24, 1929 (RG 10).

52. Photograph, "still," n.d. (RG 306).

53. Unidentified editorial, 1929 (RG 10).

54. Resolution to the Hon. Calvin Coolidge from the City Council of Baltimore, January 24, 1922 (RG 46).

55. Letter to Mr. G. W. Wickersham from A Citizen of Arkansas, July 17, 1929 (RG 10).

56. Letter to the Hon. Frank B. Kellogg from Mrs. W. C. Hair, January 6, 1926 (RG 59).

57. Letter to Miss Mabel[sic] Willebran[d]t from O. A. Calandria, n.d. (RG 60).

58. Newspaper article, *Appleton Post-Crescent*, n.d. (RG 60).

59. Letter to Mr. Henry C. Wallace from J. O. Robertson, August 14, 1922 (RG 16).

60. Cartoon, Columbus *Dispatch*, January 21, 1931 (RG 10).

61. Letter to the Hon. Herbert Hoover, President, from Alva P. Jones, May 25, 1929 (RG 10).

62. Letter to the National Law Enforcement Commission from J. M. Blough, September 10, 1929, with attachment (RG 10).

63. Letter to the Hon. George W. Wickersham from A. B. Geary, June 6, 1929 (RG 10).

64. Letter to the Hon. George W. Wickersham from George W. Dexter, June 10, 1929 (RG 10).

65. Letter to Mr. George W. Wickersham from William T. Elzinga, June 16, 1929 (RG 10).

66. Letter to the President from Arthur R. Boyden, August 5, 1929 (RG 10).

67. Letter to Crime and Law Enforcement [Commission] from John E. Ayer, M. V., May 23, 1929 (RG 10).

68. Editorial, *The Shreveport Times*, May 5, 1929 (RG 10).

69. Editorial, *The Cleveland Press*, March 13, 1928 (RG 60).

Exercise Summary Chart

EXERCISE	NUMBER OF DOCUMENTS	CONTENT	STUDENT ACTIVITIES	NUMBER OF CLASS PERIODS
1. Lifestyles in the 1920's Documents 1-5 Worksheet 1	5	Economy, technology, daily life, recreation, law enforcement	Identifying information Gathering information Classifying information	1
2. The Generation Gap Document 2	1	Technological change Cultural values	Analyzing a cartoon	1
3. A Mother's Plea Document 6	1	Intolerance, prohibition, generation gap	Analyzing a document Role-playing Letter writing	1
4. Post-War Conditions Documents 7-12	6	Issues of public concern: lynching inflation, political prisoners, farmers	Working in small groups to prepare a radio "spot"	2
5. Immigration Documents 6 and 13-17 Worksheet 2	6	American attitudes toward immigration Changes in immigration policies	Identifying and classifying attitudes Working in small groups	1 1/2
6. Farmers in the Early 1920's Document 8 Worksheet 3	1	Purchasing power of farmers, 1913-1922 Economic effects of WWI	Graphreading	1
7. Black Migration Documents 18-23	6	Factors influencing black migration to the North	Identifying point of view Making decisions Working in small groups	1 1/2 or 2
8. Language of Intolerance Documents 13, 24, and 25	3	Intolerance against blacks, Bolsheviks, immigrants	Identifying point of view and stereotypmg	1
9. Youth Documents 3, 26-28, 60, 63, and 65	7	Adolescent concerns: lynching, prohibition, education	Comparing and contrasting issues of youth in the 1920's and today Working in small groups	1 or 2

EXERCISE	NUMBER OF DOCUMENTS	CONTENT	STUDENT ACTIVITIES	NUMBER OF CLASS PERIODS
10. Youth: Attitudes Toward Moral Character Document 29 Worksheet 4	1	Teenage values	Comparing and contrasting values Identifying value statements Analyzing an opinion survey	1
11. Ku Klux Klan Documents 16 and 30-33 Worksheet 5	5	Qualification for Ku Klux Klan membership	Verifying statements using documentary evidence	1 1/2
12. Ramp Burdick Letter Document 34 Worksheet 6	1	An individual response to an experience with the Ku Klux Klan	Analyzing documents and drawing conclusions	1
13. Ku Klux Klan: Letters to the Government Documents 30, 32, and 34-38 Worksheet 7	7	Comparing points of view about the Ku Klux Klan	Identifying point of view Working in small groups Role-playing Optional creative writing assignment	1 or 2
14. The Coming of Airmail Service Documents 39-41 Worksheet 8	3	Activities of the Ku Klux Klan Presidential decisionmaking	Mapreading Testing generalizations	1
15. Changing Technology: Laundry Supplies Document 42 Worksheet 9	1	Expansion of airmail service	Locating factual evidence and drawing conclusions Comparing and contrasting domestic work in the 1920's and today	1
16. Advertising in the 1920's Documents,1,22,43, and 44	4	Home technology	Drawing conclusions from visual sources Comparing and contrasting cultural values and advertising techniques in the 1920's and today	1
17. The Equal Rights Amendment: A 1920's Perspective Documents 45 and 46 Worksheet 10	2	Advertising techniques	Developing point of view Making a decision	1

EXERCISE	NUMBER OF DOCUMENTS	CONTENT	STUDENT ACTIVITIES	NUMBER OF CLASS PERIODS
18. Working Women in the 1920's Documents 45 and 47-51 Worksheets 11 and 12	6	Concerns of working women	Graph reading Analyzing a document Comparing and contrasting the position of women in the work force between 1920 and today	1 or 2
19. Prohibition: A First Glance Documents 4, 44, 52, and 53 Worksheet 13	4	Prohibition enforcement	Locating factual information	1
20. Prohibition: Contrasting Points of View Documents 3 and 54-59	7	Public reactions to prohibition enforcement	Problem solving Comparing and contrasting points of view Working in small groups Using creative writing skills	1
21. A Cartoonist's View of Prohibition Document 60 Worksheet 14	1	Wickersham Commission findings	Analyzing a cartoon	1 or 1 1/2
22. Crime: Its Causes in the 1920's Documents 61-67	7	Causes of crime: prohibition, movies, unemployment	Comparing and contrasting evidence Using creative writing skills Working in small groups Role-playing	1
23. Attitudes Toward Justice in the 1920's Documents 68 and 69 Worksheet 15	2	Editorials on justice in the 1920's	Analyzing newspapers as primary sources Comparing and contrasting points of view	1
24. Summary Exercise	Variable	General information	Synthesizing information using creative writing skills Testing a generalization	Open-ended

Introductory Exercises

These exercises introduce students to the general objectives of the unit. They focus students' attention on documents and their importance to the historian who interprets and records the past. They serve as valuable opening exercises for this unit.

Written Document Analysis

The Written Document Analysis worksheet helps students to analyze systematically any written document in this unit. In sections 1-5 of the worksheet, students locate basic details within the document. In section 6, students analyze the document more critically as they complete items A-E. There are many possible correct answers to section 6, A-E. We suggest you use documents 6, 30, 34, or 36 with this worksheet.

The Historian's Tools

The Historian's Tools worksheet is designed to increase students' awareness of the process of analyzing historical information. It focuses on both the nature of historical sources and those factors that influence the historian's analysis of evidence. The worksheet includes specific questions on distinctions between primary and secondary sources, the reliability of those sources, and the influence of bias, point of view, and perspective on the historian's interpretation.

Students do not analyze documents to complete this worksheet as they do in other exercises in the unit. Class discussion, however, is essential to helping students understand the issues raised by the worksheet because there are many ways to answer the questions. In your discussion, stress the fact that reliability is affected by the events surrounding the creation of the document and the purposes for which the document is being evaluated. For this reason, it is essential to set documents in their historical context. Also, remind students that primary sources are not necessarily more reliable than well researched secondary sources. You may wish to assign the worksheet as homework and discuss it with students in class.

Cartoon Analysis

The Cartoon Analysis worksheet helps students to analyze systematically any cartoon in this unit. It is designed to improve students' ability to analyze the visual and written information contained in political cartoons. It can be used specifically with exercises 2 and 21.

Written Document Analysis

Worksheet

1. Type of Document (Check one):

_____ Newspaper	_____ Map	_____ Advertisement
_____ Letter	_____ Telegram	_____ Congressional record
_____ Patent	_____ Press release	_____ Census report
_____ Memorandum	_____ Report	_____ Other

2. Unique Physical Qualities of the Document (check one or more):

_____ Interesting letterhead	_____ Notations
_____ Handwritten	_____ "RECEIVED" stamp
_____ Typed	_____ Other
_____ Seals	

3. Date(s) of Document: _____

4. Author (or creator) of the Document: _____

   Position (Title): _____

5. For What Audience was the Document Written? _____

6. Document Information (There are many possible ways to answer A-E.)

   A. List three things the author said that you think are important:

      1. _____
      2. _____
      3. _____

   B. Why do you think this document was written?

      _____

      _____

   C. What evidence in the document helps you to know why it was written?
      Quote from the document.

      _____

      _____

   D. List two things the document tells you about life in the United States
      at the time it was written:

      1. _____
      2. _____

   E. Write a question to the author that is left unanswered by the document:

      _____

      _____

Designed and developed by the education staff of the National Archives and Records Administration, Washington, DC 20408.

The Historian's Tools

Worksheet

1. If you were writing a chapter in your textbook on the 1920's, list three things you would like to know about the life in that decade.

    1. _____

    2. _____

    3. _____

2. Where might you look to find information about the three topics you listed in #1?

Topic	Source of Information
_____	_____
_____	_____
_____	_____

3. Historians classify sources of information as **PRIMARY** or **SECONDARY**. Primary sources are those created by people who actually saw or participated in an event, while secondary sources are those that were created by someone either not present when that event occurred or removed from it by time. Classify the sources of information you listed in #2 as either primary or secondary by placing a **P** or **S** next to your answers in #2. Reconsider the sources you would use to find information about the 1920's; list three more here:

    1. _____

    2. _____

    3. _____

4. Some sources of historical information are viewed as more **RELIABLE** than others, though all of them may be useful. Factors such as bias, self-interest, distance, and faulty memory affect the reliability of a source. Below is a list of sources of information on the death of President Warren Harding in 1923. Rate the reliability of each source on a numerical scale in which 1 is reliable and 5 is very unreliable. Be able to support your ratings.

    A. A letter from Mrs. Harding written to the
       New York *Times* 1 week after the President's death.   1   2   3   4   5

    B. A diary entry of a Harding staff member who was
       not present at the time of the President's death.   1   2   3   4   5

C. A newspaper article written the
day after President Harding's death.   1   2   3   4   5

D. A transcript of an interview conducted with
an eyewitness 4 years after the President's death.   1   2   3   4   5

E. A high school American history textbook
description of the President's death.   1   2   3   4   5

F. A description of the President's
death in an encyclopedia.   1   2   3   4   5

5. What personal and social factors might influence historians as they write about people and
events of the past?

_____

_____

_____

6. What personal and social factors influence *you* as you read historical accounts of people
and events?

_____

_____

_____

Designed and developed by the education staff of the National Archives and Records Administration, Washington, DC 20408.

Cartoon Analysis

Worksheet

Visuals	Words (not all cartoons include words)
Step One 1. List the objects or people you see in the cartoon.	1. Identify the cartoon caption and/ or title. 2. Locate three words or phrases used by the cartoonist to identify objects or people within the cartoon. 3. Record any important dates or numbers that appear in the cartoon.
Step Two 2. Which of the objects on your list are symbols? 3. What do you think each symbol means?	4. Which words or phrases in the cartoon appear to be the most significant? Why do you think so? 5. List adjectives that describe the emotions portrayed in the cartoon.

Step Three

A.   Describe the action taking place in the cartoon.

B.   Explain how the words in the cartoon clarify the symbols.

C.   Explain the message of the cartoon.

D.   What special interest groups would agree/disagree with the cartoon's message? Why?

Designed and developed by the education staff of the National Archives and Records Administration, Washington, DC 20408.

Exercise 1
Lifestyles in the 1920's

Note to the Teacher:

This exercise is designed as an introduction to life in 1920's. Students categorize information from several sources and record their findings on worksheet 1.

Time: 1 class period

Objectives:

- To identify and classify information relating to the economy, technology, daily life, recreation, and law enforcement during the 1920's.

- To compare and contrast lifestyles between the 1920's and today.

Materials Needed:

Documents 1-5
Worksheet 1

Procedures:

1. To motivate your students, ask them to bring to class examples of consumer items that tell something about American lifestyles today. These might include objects (a cell phone, a CD), visuals (a photograph of power lines, an ad for an SUV), or written items (an article on working women, a leaflet on drug abuse). Ask students to share their items with class members and explain how their selections reflect contemporary lifestyles. As a class, discuss the following questions:

   a. Would these items together convey to a foreigner an accurate picture of American lifestyles today? Why? Why not?

   b. Are there more examples from one area of American life than another (e.g., economy, recreation, politics)? Is this significant?

   c. Does the selection of items say anything about your own values?

   d. Considering this discussion, would you select the same item again as a representative example of American lifestyles? Explain.

2. Provide a set of the four textual documents (not the photograph) to every two students in the class. Give each pair of students a copy of worksheet 1.

3. Direct students to examine each of the documents for factual information. Students should record this information under the appropriate categories on the worksheet. Remind students that every document will not supply information for all categories. Each document contains factual information for at least three categories.

4. While students work, circulate the photograph for them to examine for information to fill in on the worksheet.

5. As a culminating activity, direct students to write a summary sentence for each category on the worksheet.

6. As an alternative approach, use the five documents with the worksheet as a learning station. Display the documents or place them in a folder with the label "Changing Lifestyles in the 1920's."

Exercise 1: Lifestyles in the 1920's

Worksheet 1

	Economy	Technology	Daily life	Recreation	Law enforcement
1) Maxwell ad					
2) Cartoon "If Grandpa"					
3) Newspaper article "Girl, Boy"					
4) Metropolitan police report					
5) Photograph "Family and Radio"					

Exercise 2
The Generation Gap

Note to the Teacher:

Mass production of goods broadened the opportunities for conspicuous consumption in the United States in the 1920's. This cartoon suggests one reaction of the "older generation" to the phenomenon.

Time: 1 class period

Objectives:

- To compare and contrast cultural values between the 1920's and today.

- To identify the effects of technological change during the 1920's.

- To identify and interpret visual and written symbols in a political cartoon.

Materials Needed:

Document 2
Overhead projector
Cartoon Analysis worksheet

Procedures:

1. Make a transparency of the cartoon. Display the cartoon with an overhead projector and discuss the message of the cartoon with students. You may wish to use the Cartoon Analysis worksheet to help students interpret the cartoon's meaning.

2. The following list identifies the consumer goods pictured in the cartoon. Ask students to develop a similar list of items that would appear in a cartoon reflecting youth today. Alternatively, ask students to redesign the cartoon replacing the objects in the cartoon with appropriate objects reflecting current trends.

Movie	Streetcars	Vacuum	Money
Music	Books	Auto	Newspapers
Radio	Telephone	Icebox	Trains
Phonograph	Steam heat	School	Electric fan
Bathtub	Washing machine	Ocean liner	Stove
Electric light			

3. Discuss with students:

   a. Which of the 1920 items are seen as *necessities* today?

   b. Which of the 1920 items are no longer commonly used?

    c. How have some of the objects (auto, telephone, washing machine) changed with improved technology?

    d. What do the objects in this cartoon tell about the 1920's?

    e. Do you think your parents would say the same thing about youth today?

4. As a concluding assignment, divide the class into groups of three or four students to develop a dialogue between today's parents and youth. Direct two students in each group to assume the role of the parents and two to be the children to discuss an issue that separates them. Ask the groups to share their dialogues with other class members.

Exercise 3
A Mother's Plea

Note to the Teacher:

The Wickersham Commission, created by President Hoover in 1929, solicited information from American citizens about the causes of criminal activity during the 1920's. Thousands of citizens wrote to the commission expressing concern about the causes of crime and its increase. (See exercise 22 for some examples of these letters.)

The 1920's includes documents that reflect attitudes that may be classified as racist or ethnocentric. In this exercise, **document 6** (a letter) is typical of hundreds within the files of the National Archives and was in no way selected to encourage or perpetuate such attitudes. It was selected, as were all documents in this unit, as a reflection of the 1920's. As you use this letter, we encourage you to help students analyze it within the context of 1920's attitudes. This letter is also used in exercise 5, which includes documents that provide evidence of American attitudes toward immigrants.

Time: 1 class period

Objectives:

- To locate evidence in the document about the background of the author.

- To recognize a document as a reflection of the society in which it was created.

- To acknowledge that the generation gap is nothing new.

- To participate in a role-playing activity.

Materials Needed:

Document 6

Procedures:

1. Ask students to read the document silently or select one student to read the letter aloud while other students follow the letter on an overhead transparency or photocopy.

2. Write on the chalk board two column headings with numbers underneath, as follows:

Individual	*Society*
1. _____	1. _____
2. _____	2. _____
3. _____	3. _____

3

3. Direct students to locate, independently or as a class, evidence in the letter that gives information about the individual who has written the letter (e.g., widow, mother of teenage son, anti-Italian). Record the information on the board. Repeat the process focusing on information about the society in which the individual lived (e.g., prohibition violations, cost of alcohol, educational system). Be sure to include the significance of the "RECEIVED" stamp notation, the typed format, and the absence of a signature.

4. Review with students the information on the chalkboard in each column, discussing which is factual and which is inferred or speculated on by them.

5. As a closing activity, direct each student to draft a letter from Mr. Wickersham in reply to the mother. Be sure that students address the mother's concerns and offer a solution to her dilemma. Students should also consider whether the government should try to solve such a problem; if so, how.

6. Alternately ask students to role-play the parts of the mother, Nick, the son, and the son's companions. Direct students to re-create one of the following incidents, drawing on information from the letter and from what they know about prohibition, about life in the 1920's, and about the generation gap syndrome:

   a. The boys' decision to get a drink after swimming.

   b. The confrontation between the mother and the drunken boys.

   Follow the role-playing with a discussion of issues that can cause conflict between parents and teenagers today and ways students and their parents resolve these conflicts.

Exercise 4
Post-War Conditions

Note to the Teacher:

The 1920's began as a time of recovery from American involvement in World War I. The documents used in this exercise suggest some of the more serious concerns of Americans at the start of the decade that became known as the Roaring 20's.

Time: 2 class periods

Objectives:

- To describe issues of public concern in the United States after World War I.

- To participate effectively in small group activities.

Materials Needed:

Documents 7-12

Procedures:

1. Divide the class into five groups. Provide each group with a set of the documents.

2. Ask each group to prepare a 5-minute TV or radio spot to present to the class. The spots should describe social conditions at the opening of the new decade based on the information each group found in the documents. You may wish to discuss with students how the media they select for their presentation will affect the message and impact of that presentation.

3. We recommend the following class schedule:

   Day One — Groups read and discuss each document. They should note such details as the date the document was written, the author, and the author's purpose and possible bias. As groups prepare their spots, they should consider the following:

   a. Which situation described in the documents would you use as a lead story? Why?

   b. What human interest elements would you emphasize? How?

   c. If you included a short interview in your spot, whom might you interview? Why?

   Day Two — Groups make their final selections of the issues to be presented in their spots. The end of this class should be reserved for each group to present its spot to the class. To add reality, you may wish to videotape the group presentations.

Exercise 5
Immigration

Note to the Teacher:

During the 1920's, Congress enacted laws to limit the number of immigrants who were entering the United States. Each immigration bill established an annual ceiling for all nationalities and a system for calculating the number of each nationality to be granted entry.

In 1920, Congress passed the first legislation limiting the number of immigrants admitted to the United States. Congress used the 1910 census as the basis for determining how many immigrants from each country would be allowed to enter. The limit for each nationality was 3 percent of that nationality already living in the United States and recorded by the census takers.

In 1924, Congress passed an even more restrictive act known as the Johnson Bill, after Representative Albert Johnson of Washington, chairman of the House Committee on Immigration. The Immigration Act of 1924 established the 1890 census as the new base for determining how many immigrants would be admitted and reduced the percentage admitted to 2 percent. In fact, the foreign born population of the United States was much smaller in 1890 than in 1910, and therefore immigration was even more restricted than it would have been by a simple reduction of the base percentage. An additional effect of the 1924 act was discrimination against immigrants from Southern and Eastern European countries (Italy, Russia, and Greece) because fewer immigrants from these countries lived in the United States in 1890 than in 1910. By the end of the decade, Congress added further restrictions to those seeking entry into the United States.

With some modifications, the 1924 act remained in force for more than 40 years. The 1965 Immigration and Nationality Act replaced national quotas with annual ceilings for the Eastern and Western Hemispheres (170,000 and 120,000, respectively), with no single foreign state in the Eastern Hemisphere allowed more than 20,000 immigrants. A 1977 amendment to the 1965 act extended the 20,000-person limitation to the Western Hemisphere. The chart below displays U.S. immigration totals by year from 1920 through 1930 and by decade from 1890 through 1970.

By Year*		By Decade*	
1920	430,001	1890	455,302
1921	805,228	1900	448,572
1922	309,556	1910	1,041,570
1923	552,919	1920	430,001
1924	706,896	1930	241,700
1925	294,314	1940	70,756
1926	304,488	1950	249,187
1927	335,175	1960	265,398
1928	307,255	1970	373,326
1929	279,678		
1930	241,700		

* Figures from *Historical Statistics for the United States, Colonial Times to 1970*, U.S. Department of Commerce, Bureau of the Census, Washington, DC, 1975.

Note: To access information on succeeding decades, log onto the U.S. Census Web site at **www.census.gov.**

Time: 1-1\2 class periods

Objectives:

- To identify and classify evidence relating to American attitudes toward immigration during the 1920's.

- To describe the changes in American immigration policies during the 1920's.

- To participate effectively in small group activities.

Materials Needed:

Documents 6 and 13-17
Worksheet 2

Procedures:

1. Divide the class into five groups. Provide each group with a set of the documents and each student with a worksheet. You may wish to display document 17, the photograph of immigrant health inspections at Ellis Island, during this exercise to give students a sense of realism.

2. Direct students to complete worksheet 2 using information from the documents. As they complete the worksheet, discuss any questions they raise about the documents or immigration policies. Conclude your discussion by asking these questions:

   a. What qualifications would you require of someone wishing to immigrate to the United States?

   b. What factors do you think should be considered in establishing these qualifications?

   c. What social conditions seem to have influenced immigration policies in the United States in the 1920's?

   d. Why do you think these conditions influenced immigration policies? Which were valid considerations, in view of the events of subsequent decades?

Exercise 5: Immigration

Worksheet 2

Document date & author(s)	Author's title	Does the author favor or oppose immigration to the United States?	What reasons does the author give for his opinion?	Classify the author's reasons in one or several of these categories: a. nationalistic b. economic c. racially biased	Circle in the first column the two letters you find most convincing and explain why in the column below.

Exercise 6
Farmers in the Early 1920's

Note to the Teacher:

The document used in this exercise is a graph that represents the economic life of the average American farmer between 1913 and 1922. Using this graph will not only give your students information about the economic life of farmers in these years but will also let them practice translating visual information into their own words.

Time: 1 class period

Objectives:

- To describe American farmers' economic situation between 1913 and 1922.

- To identify the economic effects of World War I on American farmers.

- To improve graph reading skills.

Materials Needed:

Document 8
Worksheet 3

Procedures:

1. Provide a copy of the document and the worksheet to each student.

2. Review the graph briefly with students. Note the agency that created the graph, the meaning of the vertical axis (price) and horizontal axis (months of the year: January, April, July, October), and the definitions of terms in the upper left-hand corner of the graph.

3. Allow time for students to look over the document carefully and complete the worksheet. Items 1, 6, 7, 9, and 10 are false.

4. When the worksheets are complete, review the students' answers and discuss any questions they may raise. Ask students to describe and discuss briefly — either orally or in writing — the economic situation of farmers in the early 1920's. Consider with students the effects of World War I on the farmers.

Exercise 6: Farmers in the Early 1920's

Worksheet: 3

True　　**False**

_____　　_____　　1. In January 1913 the purchasing power of farm products was $300.

_____　　_____　　2. On the graph, "price" equals the average price a farmer would receive for the goods he sold, whether crops or livestock.

_____　　_____　　3. Commodities" on the chart are those goods farmers do not produce themselves; in other words, goods they have to buy.

_____　　_____　　4. "Purchasing power" represents the ratio between how much money farmers receive for their crops and livestock and how much nonfarm goods cost.

_____　　_____　　5. The difference between the highest and lowest price farmers received for their crops is $210.

_____　　_____　　6. The difference between the highest and lowest price farmers received for their crops is $210.

_____　　_____　　7. Farmers' purchasing power rose during the 1920's.

_____　　_____　　8. Farmers made more money selling their cows, pigs, and chickens in July 1919 than in July 1920.

_____　　_____　　9. In August 1922 a farmer had more money to buy a car than he did in 1913.

_____　　_____　　10. Crop prices were higher than commodity prices in August 1915, July 1917, and January 1920.

Exercise 7
Black Migration

Note to the Teacher:

Black Americans left the rural areas of the South in great numbers during World War I for the cities of the South and North. The invasion of the South by the cotton-eating boll weevil, the opening of industrial jobs vacated by enlisting soldiers, and the encouragement by the northern black press to move stimulated this migration. Although many blacks lost their new jobs to returning white soldiers and became the first victims of the economic slump that struck the nation after the war, rural residents of the South continued to leave the land seeking better opportunities.

The documents used in this exercise reveal some of the forces influencing black migration during the 1920's. The exercise will help students to weigh the impact of an individual's point of view on decision making.

Time: 1 1/2 or 2 class periods

Objectives:

- To describe the causes of black migration from the rural South during the 1920's.

- To weigh the factors that affect an individual's point of view.

- To participate effectively in small group activities.

Materials Needed:

Documents 18-23
Overhead projector
Letter from Uncle Joe to George, p. 30

Procedures:

1. Make a transparency of the letter from Uncle Joe to George. Display the letter with an overhead projector and review its content with students.

2. Below are six personality sketches. Divide the class into six groups and ask each group to assume the point of view of one of the persons described in the sketches. Provide a copy of one personality sketch to each group. Each group should select one student to represent its personality. The question to be resolved is whether or not George Johnson should accept Uncle Joe's suggestion that he move from Gordonsville, Alabama, to Cleveland, Ohio, with his wife and daughter.

7

Personality sketches:

George Johnson is 22 years old, married, and has one child age 4. He has been a tenant on Mr. Hooker's farm for 5 years.

William Johnson is George's father and Joe's brother. His age is 52 and he has been a tenant on Mr. Hooker's farm for 25 years. His wife is dead.

Mary Johnson is George's wife, age 22. She takes in Mrs. Hooker's fine laundry to make more money and is 4 months pregnant.

Walter Johnson is George's brother, age 24, a graduate of Tuskegee Institute, a teacher, and a veteran of World War I.

Joe Johnson is George's uncle who moved to Cleveland in 1919 to open a barbershop. Uncle Joe was a tenant on Mr. Hooker's farm before moving to Cleveland.

3.   Circulate the six documents to the groups to provide students with evidence of the situation George Johnson might face as he makes his decision.

4.   After students have reviewed the documents and have discussed within their groups the point of view of their characters, bring the class together and ask each group's representative to advise George on his decision. Discuss as a class the personal and social factors that influence an individual's perspective and how they compare and contrast.

5.   As a concluding assignment, direct each student to write a letter from George to Uncle Joe responding to Joe's suggestion and offering reasons for George's decision.

Cleveland, Ohio
1923

Dear George,*

Your Aunt and I have been in this city for three years. We are writing to suggest that you move here to Cleveland. This city offers good jobs at decent wages. Even though you have only worked as a farmer, a healthy young man like you should have no trouble finding work here as a laborer, carpenter, or in another trade. You and Mary and Baby Sarah could stay with us while you look for a job.

Tell your father not to worry. We will be here to help you and Cleveland is a city where a man can be a man. If cash is short, let us know and we will send you the railroad tickets.

Come soon,

Uncle Joe and Aunt Mae

*This letter was written for this exercise by the National Archives education staff.

Exercise 8
Language of Intolerance

Note to the Teacher:

Historians have characterized the 1920's as a period of increased discrimination and intolerance toward minority groups. Government agents raided "Red nests"; KKK members tarred, feathered, and lynched those who disagreed with them; southern railroad companies continued to isolate black passengers in Jim Crow cars; and individual citizens expressed anger at ethnic minorities in public and private correspondence. This exercise exposes students to selected expressions of that intolerance. The authors use such devises as sarcasm, stereotyping, name calling, and chauvinism to express their attitudes toward various groups in American society.

Time: 1 class period

Objectives:

- To define the language of intolerance and stereotyping.

- To identify and weigh the reasons for expressions of intolerance.

- To list reasons for the increase of intolerance during the 1920's.

Materials Needed:

Documents 13, 24, and 25
Overhead projector

Procedures:

1. Discuss with students the words used today to express intolerance toward individuals or groups.

2. Make an overhead transparency of each document.

3. Display each document with an overhead projector and discuss the following questions with students. Document 24 is the most direct in its intolerance, while documents 13 and 25 are more subtle expressions of intolerance.

   a. Toward what minority group is the writer expressing intolerance?

   b. Identify those words used by the writer to express his/her intolerance.

   c. What emotions does the writer suggest by his/her choice of words (e.g., anger, coldness, desperation, fear)?

   d. How would you categorize each word or term (e.g., stereotyping, name calling, chauvinism)?

   e. List any clues in the document that suggest reasons for the author's attitudes.

8

4. After looking at the documents and discussing the questions above, discuss this topic with the class: What conditions within this country in the 1920's contributed to public attitudes of intolerance toward minorities?

TELEPHONE FRANKLIN 1296

THE BLAKE MANUFACTURING CO.

SOLE MANUFACTURERS OF

VAN GLECKLAND SEMI-PORTABLE ACETYLENE
GENERATORS

SPECIAL EQUIPMENTS
LIGHT PORTABLE WELDING GENERATORS
SHOP WELDING—CUTTING GENERATORS
GENERATORS FOR RADIATOR WELDING
GENERATORS FOR LEAD BURNING

AN ABSOLUTELY SAFE ACETYLENE GENERATOR FOR ALL PURPOSES

Welding, Cutting, Lead Burning and Lighting

ADDRESS REPLIES TO
19 South Wells Street, Chicago

SPECIAL EQUIPMENTS
MANTLE BURNING LIGHTING SYSTEMS
PORTABLE CAMP OUTFITS
CONSTRUCTION FLOOD LAMPS
OXYGEN DECARBONIZERS

CHICAGO, Sept. 19, 1919

Walker D. Hines, Director General of Railroads,

United States Railroad Administration,

Washington, D. C.

Dear Sir:

The writer just returned from Elmira, N. Y. on Michigan Central Train No. 17 and was very much surprised to find that it is now becoming necessary to associate with negro passengers on a so called high grade, excess fare train.

I am sure you can appreciate the unpleasantness of being compelled to share dressing rooms with the negros.

Yours very truly,

M. W. Briggs

LISTED BY UNDERWRITERS' LABORATORIES—INSPECTED MECHANICAL APPLIANCES

Exercise 9
Youth

Note to the Teacher:

In selecting the documents for this teaching unit, we found many letters written to the government by teenagers and young adults. We included three such letters in this exercise because they reflect students' concerns during the 1920's and because we thought that they would be of special interest to students today.

Time: 1 or 2 class periods

Objectives:

- To compare and contrast the social issues of concern to adolescents and adults during the 1920's.

- To compare and contrast the issues of concern to adolescents in the 1920's and today.

- To participate effectively in small group activities.

Materials Needed:

Documents 3, 26-28, 60, 63, and 65

Procedures:

1. Assign as homework the writing of a letter to the President of the United States. In the letter, each student should express concern about a current national issue or problem (e.g., AIDS, marijuana legalization, voting procedures). The letter should suggest a role or action for the federal government to take in solving that problem, or it might argue for no action on the part of the government.

2. In class, ask students to share their letters orally with the class and to develop a list of the issues/problems of most concern to the class. Consider: What do these issues/problems tell us about teenagers today?

3. Divide the class into seven groups. Provide a set of the seven documents to each group. Allow time for the groups to read the 1920's letters and documents from and about youth in that era. As students read the documents, each group should develop two lists: one list of issues of concern as expressed by the young people, the second list of issues of concern as seen by adults.

9

4. Bring the class together to discuss the similarities and differences between the adult and youth lists. Compare and contrast the concerns of the 1920's students with the composite list of concerns of the class. Consider: What does each list tell us about students' values in the 1920's and today?

5. As a concluding assignment, direct each student to write a paragraph comparing and contrasting the concerns of young people then and now.

Girl, Boy, Bottle And Auto Most Dangerous Quartet, Says Educator

School Head Fears Destruction Of Society in Code Of Modern Youth

CHICAGO, April 18. (AP)—Edward J. Tobin, superintendent of Cook county schools and in that capacity supervisor over the schooling of 100,000 children, believes that "a young couple a bottle of moonshine and an automobile are the most dangerous quartet that can be concocted for the destruction of human society."

Tobin is one of six men, prominent in education in Cook county, who are acting as jurors in the coroner's investigation of George Lux's death early Sunday after a round of roadhouses with several other young men and girls.

His views were epitomized in six paragraphs, as follows:

About 70 percent of the young men of 18 to 25 years of age accept as the regular standard recreation a party, an auto ride, dancing and a bottle of gin or moonshine.

Bottle Dictates Habits

About 50 to 60 percent of the girls above 17 years of age accept this code.

In pre-volstead days the bottle never aspired to dictate the social habits of our young people. It does today.

A young couple, a bottle of moonshine and a automobile are the most dangerous quartet that can be concocted for the destruction of human society.

Families and homes originate from early asociation of young people of both sexes. A home or a family tied with a bottle of bootleg has a foundation in quicksand.

The bottle is a by product of prohibition, either the bottle as one of the trio has got to go or its ancestor, prohibition, must go.

The school superintendent gave it as his opinion that the liquor and delinquency problem among American youth rested first with parents, then with schools and finally with the law.

Prof. S. N. Stevens of the Department of Psychology at Northwestern, another member of the jury, expressed the opinion that no one factor is responsible for present conditions in the moral and social life of youth.

He said social instability inherited from the war was one factor; changing economic conditions and larger social freedom for women others. He touched upon the failure of parents to do their full duty, and he said that "the churches have been more interested in maintaining themselvs as institutions than in creating a larger opportunity for the development of a satisfying life on the part of their people."

As a remedy he suggested the need of recreation in the home and "a new devlopment of family interests and enthusiasms."

He said also that "youth itself must come to realize that it is the carrier of the social traditions, that in a very large measure society and civilization in the future depend upon its intellectual and moral integrity."

Exercise 10
Youth: Attitudes Toward Moral Character:

Note to the Teacher:

This exercise highlights a public opinion survey developed by the Pathfinders of America during the 1920's. To stimulate student interest, we have modified the survey form to appear as worksheet 4. The worksheet allows students to compare and contrast their opinions with those of adolescents in the 1920's.

Time: 1 class period

Objectives:

- To compare and contrast teenage moral values in the 1920's and today.

- To draw conclusions based on information in an opinion survey.

Materials Needed:

Document 29
Worksheet 4
Overhead projector

Procedures:

1. Worksheet 4 is adapted from document 29. Provide each student with a copy of the worksheet. Instruct each student to answer the questions on the worksheet by circling yes or no or by marking the response that most nearly reflects his or her own opinion.

2. Make a transparency of document 29. When students have completed the worksheet, display the transparency with an overhead projector to the class, and compare and contrast the attitudes revealed by the survey with the students' responses. Ask a student to tally the class responses and compare the percentages with the 1924 survey totals.

3. As a concluding assignment, direct each student to summarize the class discussion in a paragraph that describes his or her sense of the moral values of students in 1924 and today.

4. As an alternate conclusion, direct students to work individually or in small groups to redesign the survey to reflect contemporary language and attitudes. Compare and contrast the students' survey with that of the Pathfinders.

Exercise 10: Youth Attitudes Toward Moral Character

Worksheet 4

Excerpts from a Questionnaire relative to Moral Problems in the
High Schools as judged by the students, North Central Association
of Colleges and Schools, covering 19 States. Edited by Prof. C.O.
Davis, University of Michigan, Ann Arbor, Michigan.

The chief moral qualities exhibited by
pupils:
    Honesty _____
    Fellowship _____
    Clean habits _____
    Courtesy lowest with only _____

The most regrettable practices of boys in
school:
    Smoking _____
    Swearing _____
    Drinking _____
    Telling vulgar stories _____

The most regrettable practices of girls in
school:
    Cosmetics _____
    Flirting & petting _____
    Profane language _____

Factors tending to develop high moral
qualities among pupils:
    Teacher _____
    School Organization _____
    Athletics _____

Invidious factors tending to undermine
right conduct:
    Certain low minded people _____
    Poor discipline _____
    Immoral parties _____

How could school help to develope morality
among pupils?
    Course in morals _____
    Stricter Rules _____
    Talks _____

Is a course in moral education desirable?
    _____ "Yes"
    _____ "No"

Some forces which are the most helpful:
    Mother _____
    Father _____
    Teacher _____

Influences which made pupils do what they
should not have done:
    Evil companions _____
    Personal weakness _____
    Immoral movies _____
    Wish to be popular & desire
    for a good time _____

High school ambitions:
    To be all around capable person _____
    Excellent student _____

Things pupils are proud of:
    The High School spirit _____
    Athletic Activities _____
    Moral strength _____

What change in class procedure advocated:
    More class discussions _____
    More recitations by pupils _____
    More explanations _____

Things making a boy popular:
    Athletics _____
    Scholarship _____
    Good looks _____
    Dependability has _____
    Capability only _____
    Character only _____

Things that make a girl popular:
    Appearance _____
    Scholarship _____
    Personality _____
    Morality _____
    Character _____

What would you expect to learn from a
course in marriage, home & parenthood?
    How to make married
    life a success _____
    Sex instruction
    (what it is all about) _____
    Parenthood _____

Characteristics of an ideal boy:
    Education _____
    Good morals _____
    Athletics _____

Characteristics of an ideal girl:
    Honesty _____
    Education _____
    Good looks _____
    Morality Capability _____

Present causes of worry:
    Choice of vocation _____
    Money matters _____
    Studies _____
    Religious matters _____

Future life problems:
    Marriage _____
    Money _____
    Vocation _____
    Service _____

Admission from pupils of using
vulgar or profane language:
    Yes _____   No _____

Flying into fits of violent temper:
    Yes _____   No _____

Telling or willingly listening to
vulgar stories:
    Yes _____   No _____

Note: That a goodly number of pupils regret the fact that the full meaning
of life is not made clear to them by the school.

Pathfinders of America, Human Engineers,
311 Lincoln Bldg., Detroit, Mich.

Exercise 11
Ku Klux Klan

Note to the Teacher:

Through the years the Ku Klux Klan advocated white supremacy. But the "new" Klan, established in 1915 by William Simms and flourishing in the 1920's, expanded its focus beyond this single issue. The Klan's view of true "Americanism" excluded Roman Catholics, Jews, and non-English-speaking immigrants as well as blacks.

In this exercise, students complete a diagnostic test (worksheet 5) on the 1920's Ku Klux Klan before examining five documents to locate evidence that supports or negates their answers. Note that in document 31 the word "tenants" is a misspelling of "tenets."

Time: 1-1/2 class periods

Objectives:

- To identify the qualifications for membership in the Ku Klux Klan.

- To correct student misconceptions about the Klan.

Materials Needed:

Documents 16 and 30-33
Worksheet 5

Procedures:

1. Provide each student with a copy of worksheet 5 and allow time for them to complete it.

2. Make enough copies of the five documents for each student to have a copy of at least one document. Students should exchange copies until they have read each of the five documents.

3. Direct students to read each document and look for evidence to confirm or refute their answers on the worksheet. In the space below each of the 10 statements, students should identify the number of the document(s) in which they found the evidence, then correct their incorrect statements.

4. As a concluding activity, ask each student to use the information gained to write a short paragraph summarizing the qualifications for Klan membership. As an alternative, instruct each student to write three accurate pieces of information about the Ku Klux Klan in the 1920's based on evidence obtained from the documents.

Exercise 11: Ku Klux Klan

Worksheet 5

Directions: Check either "True" or "False" in the column to the left of each statement.

True   **False**

_____   _____   1. Ku Klux Klan membership was secret.

_____   _____   2. The Klan existed only in southern states.

_____   _____   3. The Ku Klux Klan encouraged new immigrants to join.

_____   _____   4. The Klan promoted interracial harmony.

_____   _____   5. Many Roman Catholics were members of the Klan.

_____   _____   6. The Klan encouraged its members to buy from Jewish store owners.

_____   _____   7. Women could join the Ku Klux Klan.

_____   _____   8. Klan literature emphasized Christian religious doctrines.

_____   _____   9. Klan members believed in the U.S. Constitution.

_____   _____   10. The Klan recruited only persons born in the United States.

Exercise 12
Rampy Burdick Letter

Note to the Teacher:

Because Ku Klux Klan violence increased during the 1920's, hundreds of citizens appealed to the federal government to put an end to this activity in their communities. The letter used with this exercise is typical of the many requests for government intervention. Other exercises in this teaching unit describe in greater detail the role of the Klan in the North and South. This exercise focuses on the emotional tension created by the Klan activity within a community and one citizen's reaction to this tension.

Time: 1 class period

Objectives:

- To identify language that expresses an individual's emotional response to an incident involving the Ku Klux Klan.

- To empathize with individuals living in the past.

Materials Needed:

Document 34
Worksheet 6

Procedures:

1. Provide each student with copies of document 34 and worksheet 6.

2. The language of the document will be difficult for some students. We suggest you review the meaning of these words with your students: guise, furrow, copse, felons, foiled, Sovietism, dastardly, outrage, curs, discretion, and supplicate.

3. When the worksheets are completed, discuss with students the incident described in the document and review the nature of their reactions to the incident. Consider: Do you think such incidents occur in the United States today? What role do you think the government should play in such incidents?

Exercise 12: Rampy Burdick Letter

Worksheet 6

1. Describe what happened to the Burdick family.

2. Locate the words in the letter that are evidence of Rampy Burdick's feelings about what happened to this family. Write those words here:

3. Describe the role of the local and state government in aiding the Burdick family.

4. How do you think Attorney General Sargeant might have answered this letter?

5. If you were to face a similar situation, describe how you think you might feel or react. How might you seek help? What assistance or response would you expect from the government?

Exercise 13
Ku Klux Klan: Letters to the Government

Note to the Teacher:

During the 1920's, many citizens wrote to Presidents Harding and Coolidge and to the Department of Justice about the Ku Klux Klan. This exercise uses six of these letters to provide students with information about Klan activity during the 1920's. You may limit this exercise to procedure 1 (a worksheet activity). Procedures 2 and 3 constitute a role-playing exercise that builds on procedure 1 and requires an additional class period.

You may wish to display the photograph of President Coolidge (**document 35**) during this exercise so that students can consider what the White House atmosphere might have been at the time.

Time: 1 or 2 class periods

Objectives:

- To describe the activities of the Ku Klux Klan during the 1920's.

- To outline a federal government policy toward the Klan appropriate to conditions in the 1920's.

- To describe some factors influencing presidential decision making.

- To work effectively in small group and role-playing activities.

Materials Needed:

Documents 30, 32, and 34-38
Worksheet 7

Procedures:

1. Divide the class into six groups. Give each group a copy of one of the letters and provide a copy of worksheet 7 to each group member. Ask one volunteer in each group to read the letter to the other group members. Encourage students to discuss the content of the letter and to fill in their worksheets together.

2. Announce to the class that they will participate in a role-playing activity that uses the information in their letters. The setting is President Coolidge's office at the White House. The date is early 1928. The President, in an effort to learn more about the Ku Klux Klan, has invited the authors of the six letters to meet with him. He has told the persons involved that they each will have 3 minutes to speak with him about the Klan.

   a. Ask each group to select one of its members to send to the White House meeting. The remaining group members will serve as advisors to help the speaker prepare the most important information for the talk. Allow approximately 5 minutes for students to confer with their selected envoy.

b. Request that a volunteer serve as President Coolidge. As President, he or she will serve chiefly as a listener rather than as a discussant.

c. Each of the six speakers will talk with the President for the allotted time. The other class members should take notes on the information presented. After all the speakers have finished, the class will serve as the President's brain trust of advisors to help him formulate an official position on the Ku Klux Klan.

Before students begin this process, remind them that presidential decisions are often the result of complex influences rather than one-dimensional. Pressure from interest groups, information from advisors, economic and political realities, and public input — all affect a President's policymaking. Ask students to speculate about the forces that may have influenced Coolidge's position on the Ku Klux Klan.

3. As an extended activity, direct students to do one of the following:

a. Instruct them to return to their groups to formulate an official White House statement about the Ku Klux Klan. Each group's statement should be approximately four sentences in length.

b. As an alternative, each student might prepare a statement for the President, or the class together, with the teacher as moderator, might prepare an official position statement.

c. Direct each student to write a letter in reply to one of the six letters as the President or the Department of Justice might have answered it. The letter should include a specific answer to the writer's request, even if the answer is simply a statement that little can be done.

198589

Chas. D. Levy
WHOLESALE
DRY GOODS
OFFICES AND SALESROOMS
1444 ~ 1450 St. Clair Avenue
CLEVELAND   OHIO
June 24th, 1924.

Honorable Calvin Coolidge,
        President of the United States,
        Washington, D. C.

My Dear Mr. President:

        I have been a staunch Republican for many
years, casting my first vote for James A. Garfield.

        I have twenty-three Department Stores lo-
cated throughout the different towns and cities of Ohio.
In some of these towns and cities the Ku Klux Klan organization has placed a boycott on several of my stores, on
account of me being fortunate enough to be born a Hebrew,
and just as soon as the present leases expire I will be
compelled to move from these sections.

        In the town of Ashland, Ohio, where one of my
stores is located, there was held a meeting in the Public
Square, and in front of thousands of spectators who had
gathered to hear the speakers, the Ku Klux Klan openly
told the audience they should not patronize any Jewish
merchant. I think this is just plain boycott and very un-
fair to an American citizen or even a Non-American citizen.

        I have read your platform and taken special
notice to the paragraph in which you state that you demand
"law and order" and "the protection of all citizens."

        All I am asking for is your protection in this
matter. If you have promised it for the next four years
there is no reason why you cannot give it to us now, as you
are The President now, of this glorious country, the same
as I hope you will be for the next four years.

        I await your kind reply for which I thank you
in advance.

                        Very sincerely,

CDL/N

Exercise 13: Ku Klux Klan: Letters to the Government

Worksheet 7

1. Name of the letter writer: _____

   Location: _____

   Date of letter: _____

2. What does the letter tell you about the Ku Klux Klan? (activities, policies, etc.)

3. Why do you think the letter was written?

4. What does the author want the government to do?

5. Government letter in reply (procedure 3C):

   Date: _____

   Address of person written to: _____

   Dear: _____

   _____

   _____

   _____

   _____

   _____

   _____

   _____

   _____

   (Continue on back)

Exercise 14
The Coming of Airmail Service

Note to the Teacher:

In 1918 Post Office pilots flying War Department planes began to deliver mail between New York City and Washington, DC, with a stop in Philadelphia. Later in the year, the Post Office assumed complete direction of airmail service between New York City and Washington, and by 1924 the Post Office offered to the public airmail service between New York City and San Francisco, CA. The Air Mail Act of 1925 established a contract system whereby private companies provided airmail service along routes that connected with the government-operated transcontinental route. Reflecting the rapid expansion of airmail use, the price for an ounce of mail dropped from 10¢ per half ounce in 1927 to 5¢ an ounce by 1928. You may wish to display the photograph of Lindbergh's inaugural airmail flight to add a sense of realism to the study of the growth of airmail service (**document 39**).

Time: 1 class period

Objectives:

- To describe the growth of airmail service in the 1920's.
- To develop map reading skills.
- To test a generalization.

Materials Needed:

Documents 39-41
Worksheet 8

Procedures:

1. Read aloud to the class the following generalizations concerning airmail service in the late 1920's. You may wish to write these on the chalkboard while students complete the worksheet.

   a. The expansion of airmail service greatly improved communication between the regions of the United States during the 1920's.

   b. The addition of air service by the Post Office Department in the 1920's reflected the growing American interest in the airplane.

   c. Private control of airmail routes stimulated the expansion of airmail service in the 1920's.

2. Provide each student with a copy of each map and the worksheet.

3. Allow students time to study the maps and to complete the worksheet.

4. Review the worksheet answers with students and consider which of the three generalizations are best supported by the documentation provided in this exercise. What information would help you to weigh the accuracy of these three generalizations?

Exercise 14: The Coming of Airmail Service

Worksheet 8

Directions: Study the maps of 1926 and 1928 to answer the following questions.

1. What do the solid black lines on the maps represent?

2. In 1926, were there more airmail routes from east to west or from north to south?

3. To what foreign country could you send an airmail letter in 1926? 1928?

4. In 1928, a letter sent from Washington, DC, to Atlanta, GA, would pass through several cities. List them.

5. Would your letter have traveled by airmail ?

	1926		1928	
from Chicago, IL, to Nashville, TN?	Yes	No	Yes	No
from New York City to Cleveland, OH?	Yes	No	Yes	No
from San Francisco, CA, to Salt Lake City, UT?	Yes	No	Yes	No
from Atlanta, GA, to Miami, FL?	Yes	No	Yes	No
from Fargo, ND, to Lincoln, NE?	Yes	No	Yes	No

6. Which major north to south airmail route was not proposed in 1926 but was in operation by 1928?

7. Why do you think airmail service existed between cities as close to each other as New York and Philadelphia?

8. Speculate on areas in the country where airmail routes would be added by 1930.

9. Estimate the distance of Lindbergh's airmail delivery route between St. Louis, MO, and Chicago, IL. _____ miles

Exercise 15
Changing Technology: Laundry Supplies

Note to the Teacher:

Many new labor-saving devices for the home became available during the 1920's. Among these products were electric washing machines, irons, vacuum cleaners, and refrigerators. Through this exercise, students will become aware of the technological changes that affected the domestic life of many Americans by the late 1920's. **Document 42** illustrates the type of laundry supplies sold in 1922-23 by Montgomery Ward. Electric washing machines are not included for sale in this document; however, they were available for purchase at this time from Montgomery Ward. An example of an early electric washing machine, described in **document 43**, may be useful for comparing prices and changes in domestic technology.

Time: 1 class period

Objectives:

• To recognize the impact of technological change in the home since the 1920's.

• To compare and contrast domestic work in the 1920's with domestic work today.

Materials Needed:

Document 42
Worksheet 9

Procedures:

1. Provide each student with a copy of document 42 and worksheet 9.

2. When students have completed the worksheet, ask them to discuss the following question:

   How do you think technology will change household work in the future?

   Students should consider the impact of nuclear and solar power, microwaves, laser beams, home computers, and synthetic fabrics on domestic life.

Exercise 15: Changing Technology: Laundry Supplies

Worksheet 9

Directions: Answer the following questions from information in document 42.

1. How many types of irons are for sale? Compare and contrast the special features and prices of these irons.

2. How much would 300 feet of twisted clothesline wire cost?

3. As far as you know, which items are no longer being sold? List them.

4. What item is made of a substance that is now considered a health hazard?

5. What would be the total cost of the following items ordered from the list of laundry supplies?

	COST
1 brass washboard	_____
100 feet of solid clothesline	_____
12 dozen spring-pin clothespins	_____
1 charcoal iron	_____
Total:	_____

6. List three ways that electricity has changed the process of cleaning clothes since 1922.
   1. _____
   2. _____
   3. _____

7. The following prices are listed in the 1979 Montgomery Ward catalog:

1922-23	INCREASE
Ironing board cover ($7.99)	_____
Ironing board ($22.99)	_____
Irons ($ 12.95-31.95)	_____
Wall-mount clothesline reel ($11.49)	_____

   In the space to the right, indicate the price of the same item in the 1922-23 catalog. How much has the item increased in cost since 1922-23?

8. You are setting up a 1922-23 household and have budgeted $10.00 for laundry supplies, which you plan to purchase from Montgomery Ward. List the items you need and could afford within this budget. Include the price of each item and total the cost below.

Exercise 16
Advertising in the 1920's

Note to the Teacher:

During the 1920's, advertising became a more sophisticated aspect of business. Commercial firms spent large sums to study the psychology of consumer buying. In addition, they encouraged consumers to spend more by offering attractive credit incentives. In this exercise, students will examine four documents that are typical of 1920's advertisements.

Time: 1 class period

Objectives:

- To compare and contrast advertising techniques of the 1920's with those of today.

- To compare and contrast cultural values between the 1920's and today.

Materials Needed:

Documents 1, 22, 43, and 4

Procedures:

1. As background for this exercise, instruct students to bring a current advertisement to class. In class, discuss the techniques used by the advertiser to encourage the reader to buy the product. List these techniques on the board. In discussion, consider how the ad reflects current American cultural values.

2. Make copies or a transparency of each of the four documents for students to examine. As students look at the ads, they should answer the following questions:

    a. What product is the advertiser trying to sell?

    b. Who is the intended audience for each ad? What clues help you decide?

    c. Make a list of the selling points used by the advertiser to make the product appealing. Would these same selling points be important to today's consumer? Explain your reasons.

    d. Which ads offer credit buying plans? Describe the terms.

3. As a concluding discussion or a short written assignment, ask students to consider the following questions:

    a. After reviewing advertisements of both the 1920's and today, to what extent do you think they reflect American cultural values?

b. If you knew nothing about American culture and looked only at these four ads, what would you identify as the cultural values and interests of Americans in the 1920's? How do these values and interests compare and contrast to those you would identify in current advertisements?

c. Do you think that these advertisements are an accurate reflection of American cultural values? Explain.

d. What selling points do you think advertisers might feature in future ads? Explain.

4. Extended activities:

a. Ask students to choose four advertisements from the class contributions that they think best represent current American values.

b. Select several current ads for cars, washing machines, or real estate. Direct students to compare and contrast the selling points of each of the 1920's products with today's ad for the same or similar product. Ask students to consider how the ads reflect changes in American cultural values.

Are You Getting Your Share of the Country's Prosperity?
OTHERS ARE, WHY NOT YOU?

We have made many people independent by establishing them in their own homes at our beautiful developments. Let us do the same for you.

The Hegemonian can be built from $1,250 up. Payable $12.50 monthly.

Own your own home, pay for it with your rent at New Brunswick Terrace on the Main Line Pennsylvania Railroad, near the large industrial city of New Brunswick, 55 minutes' ride from New York City, the most prosperous city in the world, and also a short ride from Philadelphia.

HIGH WAGE SCALE EQUAL RIGHTS AND OPPORTUNITIES

You will not be congested or crowded into slums of large cities or towns where race riots and prejudice are bred. Secure some of our desirable building lots, on easy payments.

When the land is paid for you can have your own home built according to your requirements from $1250 up, payable $12.50 monthly.

If you have any regard for your own or your family's future, do not miss this opportunity.

Last Call for Lots at a Special Price

$69
EACH

Prices on all lots positively increased November 1st.

Send for free illustrated booklet showing modern homes built by us and occupied by Colored people.

HEGEMAN HOMES

The N. T. HEGEMAN COMPANY
We are open for several keen and progressive representatives on salary and commission basis.

Main Office, 9 Church Street, New York City

Exercise 17
The Equal Rights Amendment: A 1920's Perspective

Note to the Teacher:

The focus of the women's movement shifted as social and political attitudes changed in America during the first two decades of the 20th century. Before World War I, most members of women's organizations were social feminists; that is, they sought social justice for women and disadvantaged people. They fought for child welfare legislation, pure food and drug acts, conservation, and other regulations that would control the rapid industrialization and urbanization of American life. With the coming of the war, many women shifted their energies to supporting the war effort on the home front and uniting efforts to gain the right to vote.

With the passage of the 19th amendment in 1920, the feminists appeared to lose their sense of common purpose and unity. Most women continued to support social feminism, concentrating on general social reforms with particular emphasis on laws that discriminated against women. A smaller group of women transferred their attention to passage of the equal rights amendment. Led by Alice Paul and the national Woman's Party, they argued that passage of an equal rights amendment to the Constitution was the best way to end the numerous and contradictory state and national laws that discriminated against women.

The Equal Rights Amendment (ERA) was formally introduced in Congress by the Woman's Party in 1923. The amendment stated simply that "men and women shall have equal rights throughout the United States and every place subject to its jurisdiction." Supporters viewed ERA as a vehicle to end legal strictures against women in areas such as marriage and property holding. A special target of the Woman's Party was the elimination of state protective industrial laws for women. These laws affected some 4 million female workers in 42 of the 43 states in the union. Laws limited the workweek for women to 48 or 54 hours in 25 states, prohibited night work in 16 states, and required a minimum wage for women in 13 states.

Proponents of ERA argued that state protective laws limited opportunities for working women in several ways: women could not compete for better paying night jobs and could lose seniority and chances for administrative positions that demanded longer hours or night work. Night work restrictions in some states, for example, limited the opportunities for females as printers, railway conductors, or pharmacists. When a 60-hour workweek was not uncommon, the 48-hour law excluded women in many states from taking jobs such as drill, lathe, and textile machine operators.

While the states' protective laws varied, proponents of ERA pointed to general wage inequities between men and women in the same jobs. One 1927 study of 1,600 industrial establishments confirmed these inequities: The average weekly wage for all male workers was $29.35 whereas the average weekly wage for all female workers was $17.34.

While the Woman's Party strongly supported ERA, many other groups of women, including the League of Women Voters and the National Women's Trade Union League, opposed such legislation. They viewed state protective legislation for industrial women, much of which had been passed between 1911 and 1921, as an important gain for working women. The supporters of this legislation cited significant improvements in work conditions in those states that had established legal standards for women. They pointed with pride to the increased employment opportunities for women documented by the 1920 census. They argued that the legislation protected the health of the female worker, who was often burdened with the two jobs of mother and wage earner. In addition, they noted that the hour laws brought the hours of working women more nearly in line with the average workweek of the male worker, while the wage laws helped to establish minimum wage standards for women.

In this exercise, students read a letter from one group of women in the 1920's who argued against the equal rights amendment. Students will examine the letter and make a decision either to support or not to support the 1923 amendment.

Time: 1 class period

Objectives:

- To describe the concerns of women, especially working women, during the 1920's.

- To list the effects of ERA on women in the 1920's.

Materials Needed:

Documents 45 and 46
Worksheet 10
Overhead projector

Procedures:

1. As a homework assignment, direct students to complete the opinion survey (worksheet 10).

2. Make a transparency of document 45 or provide copies of the document to students. Cover the dates in the letter (top of page and line 3) and direct students to guess the date of the document. Discuss their reasons for selecting these dates.

3. Ask students to make a list of arguments/reasons stated by the authors to support their position on ERA. Encourage students to agree or disagree with each point and to discuss their reasons. Include students' worksheet responses in the discussion.

4. Make an overhead transparency of the 1923 Equal Rights Amendment. After the students read the document, discuss with them the possible impact of ERA on working women in the 1920's. Ask students to imagine themselves as citizens living in 1923 and to vote either for or against the 1923 equal rights amendment. Encourage students to consider what additional information they would need to make an informed decision on this issue.

5. Extended activities:

    a. Ask students to research the history of ERA after the 1920's. Encourage them to investigate how the arguments of opponents and proponents of the amendment changed over time. Ask them to consider how these arguments reflected the changing status of working women.

    b. Direct students to locate pictures and articles in recent periodicals that describe nontraditional jobs for women and men. Students could make a display of the pictures and report to the class about career information.

I7

Exercise 17: The Equal Rights Amendment: A 1920's Perspective

Worksheet 10

Directions: Answer the following questions, justifying your answer in one or more sentences:

YES   NO

_____   _____   1.   Do you think women need special protection on the job?
List two reasons why or why not.

_____   _____   2.   Do you think there are some jobs that men do better than women?

_____   _____   3.   Do you think employers should consider the sex of the applicant
when hiring? Why or why not.

_____   _____   4.   Do you think motherhood affects women as workers?

Exercise 18
Working Women in the 1920's

Note to the Teacher:

Women entered the work force in large numbers during World War I, often replacing men who were serving in the military. They filled a variety of skilled jobs, working as drill press operators, streetcar conductors, and government clerks. In the postwar period, an additional two million women entered the job market, leading many historians to conclude that World War I widened opportunities for women. In reality, employers fired or demoted many working women when the war ended. With the exception of new clerical opportunities and jobs in the automobile and iron industries, women made few real gains in the labor force during the 1920's. From 1920 to 1930, the percentage of working women in the work force increased only 1 percent, from 23 percent to 24 percent.

The documents in this exercise provide glimpses into the lives of working women in the 1920's. The documents do not offer information about professional women, who were 96 percent of all nurses, 88 percent of all librarians, and 62 percent of all social workers. In other professions, their numbers were fewer: only 1.4 percent of lawyers and 5 percent of doctors were women, and women made up less than 1 percent of all mathematicians and physicists.

You may wish to limit this exercise to procedure 1. Should you include procedure 2, students examine five additional documents and complete an additional worksheet.

Time: 1 or 2 class periods

Objectives:

- To compare and contrast the position of women in the work force between 1920 and today.

- To recognize the influence of historical perspective on conclusions drawn from evidence.

- To improve graph reading skills.

Materials Needed:

Documents 45 and 47-51
Worksheets 11 and 12
Current Department of Labor statistical information for working women from the agency's Web site, **www.dol.gov**

Procedure 1

1. Provide a copy of worksheet 11 to each student. Ask students to answer (in the left-hand column) the questions from the perspective of a working woman of the 1920's.

2. After students have answered the questions, provide them with a copy of the graphs, document 47. Using information from the graphs, direct students to correct their answers.

3. Ask students to answer (in the right-hand column) the questions from the perspective of a working woman of today.

4. Review student answers to the questions and provide them with current statistical information from the Department of Labor Web site at **www.dol.gov** related to the following topics:

   a. Percentage of single, widowed, and divorced women in the work force.

   b. Percentage of women employed in clerical, domestic/service work, professional and technical work.

   c. Percentage of working women in various age groups.

   d. Percentages of female workers as compared to male workers.

5. Discuss with students the difference in their answers in the left-hand and right-hand columns. Ask them to speculate on the factors that may have resulted in the most significant changes they discern.

Procedure 2

1. Divide students into small groups; provide a copy of worksheet 12 to each student and copies of documents 45, 47, 49, and 50 to each group; and circulate documents 48 and 51 among the groups. Direct students to complete the worksheet using information from all six documents.

2. As a homework assignment, instruct students to write a short paragraph (3-5 sentences) in which they answer the following question using information from the documents.

   What advantages do working women have today that they did not have in the 1920's?

   As an alternative, lead a class discussion focusing on this question.

Exercise 18: Working Women in the 1920's

Worksheet 11

Directions: Imagine yourself as a typical woman living in the 1920's and answer the questions below in the left-hand column. Answer the questions again in the right-hand column as you think they would be answered by a typical working woman of today.

	1920	Today

1. If you worked, would you likely be:
 	
  a. Married
 	
  b. Single		

2. Which of these jobs would you most likely perform?
 	
  a. Service work (domestic)
 	
  b. Clerical work
 	
  c. Professional or technical work		

3. As a working woman, in what age group would you most likely be?
 	
  a. 16-19 years
 	
  b. 20-44 years
 	
  c. over 44 years		

4. All female workers together would be approximately what percentage of the total labor force?
 	
  a. 20%
 	
  b. 40%
 	
  c. 60%		

McLean County Unit #5
201-EJHS

18

Exercise 18: Working Women in the 1920's

Worksheet 12

Directions: After examining the six documents, what have you learned about working women in the 1920's? Complete the following, using information from the documents.

1. What percentage of women were employed in all occupations?

2. Identify the one occupation in which more women than men were employed.

3. List the three occupational categories in which most women worked.

   1. _____

   2. _____

   3. _____

4. Name the family member to whom most advertising was directed.

5. Name the family member who was expected to wash clothing.

6. Approximately how many women were employed in industry in 1924?

7. List three types of state legislation aimed at protecting women industrial workers.

   1. _____

   2. _____

   3. _____

8. List two reasons why the Connecticut Council of Catholic Workers opposed the proposed equal rights amendment.

   1. _____

   2. _____

9. Briefly describe the clothing worn by many working women.

10. Briefly describe the hairstyle of many working women.

11. According to Dr. A. M. Young, a girl arriving in New York City to look for a job should have had how much money?

12. List three glamorous jobs sought by women in New York City.

   1. _____

   2. _____

   3. _____

13. List two problems encountered by women who went to New York City to look for a job.

   1. _____

   2. _____

14. Why did Cooper, Wells & Co. build dormitories for its female workers?

15. Calculate the difference between the weekly cost of room and board for a working girl in New York City and a working girl at the Cooper, Wells & Co. hosiery plant.

Exercise 19
Prohibition: A First Glance

Note to the Teacher:

In this exercise, students examine three documents about violations of the prohibition amendment. You may wish to display the photograph of the government raid of a still to stimulate student interest in this controversial issue.

Time: 1 class period

Objectives:

- To describe life in the United States during the 1920's.
- To recognize the difficulty of enforcing prohibition during the 1920's.

Materials Needed:

Documents 4, 44, 52, and 53
Worksheet 13
Overhead projector

Procedures:

1. Provide a worksheet for each student and allow time for students to read it carefully.

2. Make a transparency of each of the three textual documents.

3. Students will need to know the meaning of these words to complete the worksheet:

prohibition	fusillade	violation
intoxicating	contraband	
invigorating	customs	

4. Display each of the three textual documents with an overhead projector, allowing time for students to examine them carefully. Instruct students to identify the document that contains information to verify each statement on the worksheet.

5. After showing all three textual documents, project each one again briefly for those students who have missed a statement or want to check their answers.

6. Ask individual students to supply the correct answers to each statement while all students check their answers.

7. Use the documents as a vehicle for discussing the following questions:

    a. What role did the government play in enforcing prohibition?

    b. Did the public support the 18th Amendment?

    c. What other information would you need to weigh the effectiveness of prohibition?

Exercise 19: Prohibition: A First Glance

Worksheet 13

Directions: The following are facts about life in the United States during the 1920's. You can locate evidence to support each statement in one of the three textual documents. In the space to the left of each item, fill in an appropriate abbreviation for each source if it applies to that statement.

Brumalt Ad   Editorial   Police Report

_____   1. The police arrested many citizens for drinking too much during the 1920's.

_____   2. There was smuggling of alcohol from Canada to the United States.

_____   3. It cost a little less than 1¢ to make a glass of home brew.

_____   4. Enforcement of prohibition laws could lead to violence.

_____   5. Companies advertised ways to violate the 18th amendment.

_____   6. Barley malt, a capper, caps, and selected hops are among the items needed to make beer at home.

_____   7. Some papers published editorials to protest the use of violent methods to enforce prohibition.

_____   8. In 1922, the police of Vincennes, IN, arrested more citizens for breaking liquor laws than any other law.

Exercise 20
Prohibition: Contrasting Points of View

Note to the Teacher:

In this activity, students examine letters and visual materials that document the national discussion of prohibition. From 1918 to 1933, concerned citizens and interest groups wrote to the government to offer suggestions and to express their views on prohibition and its enforcement. These documents illustrate the complexity of public sentiment on this national issue.

Time: 1 class period

Objectives:

- To identify an individual's point of view regarding prohibition.

- To comprehend the difficulty of enforcing prohibition during the 1920's.

- To compare and contrast issues defined as controversial in the 1920's and today.

- To participate effectively in small group activities.

Materials Needed:

Documents 3 and 54-59

Procedures:

1. Ask the class to select one currently controversial social issue to investigate. Ask students to bring to class newspaper or magazine articles or editorials on the issue. Give students several days to collect their articles. Ask them to summarize the author's point of view on the issue and to locate evidence the author uses to support his or her conclusion. On an assigned day, discuss with the class the variety of viewpoints they have found on the issue. After analyzing several of the articles, ask the class to write a definition for the term "point of view."

2. Divide students into groups of five or six and give each group one of the seven documents about prohibition. Ask them to read the document and complete the following:

   a. Summarize the author's point of view on prohibition enforcement.

   b. Locate evidence in the document to support your answer to "A."

   c. Does the author include any issues other than prohibition enforcement in the document? If so, list those issues.

3. Ask each group to summarize for the class the information in its document about prohibition enforcement. Discuss each author's point of view on this issue. In two columns, list on the board the issues and viewpoints.

4. As a culminating activity, ask each student to write a paragraph in response to the question below. The paragraph should include information from the documents read in class as well as the student's own opinion.

> If you had been a citizen living in the 1920's, what would you have suggested to the government as a practical plan to deal with the complex issue of prohibition enforcement?

reach a verdict.

A Sign and a Shot

Border patrolmen have been trying to halt the smuggling of liquor from Canada into Minnesota. It is a regulation, that when they set up a sign along a road, cars driving past must halt to be searched. Last Saturday a car containing a man, his wife and two children drove past such a sign near International Falls. According to the wife—who became a widow immediately afterward—they were driving slowly and were not yet entirely past the sign when a fusillade of bullets swept the car. The bullets were fired without warning and one of them struck the husband in the back of the neck, killing him instantly. An examination of the car showed no contraband. "I only did my duty," said the border patrol who fired into a family party.

Had he suspected the driver of being merely a bank robber, or perhaps a fugitive murderer, we doubt if he would have raked with his shotgun a car in which obviously there were innocent persons riding. But because he suspected that a quart or perhaps a gallon or two, of liquor was passing, he "shot to kill" to quote a customs order alleged to have been issued from Duluth. This was just one of those things that happen under prohibition.

A Province of the Hills

Exercise 21
A Cartoonist's View of Prohibition

Note to the Teacher:

By 1929, it was evident that enforcement of the 18th Amendment was ineffective. President Herbert Hoover, in response to public demand and his own personal convictions, appointed a commission to study the problems of law enforcement, with particular emphasis on prohibition. Hoover designated former Attorney General George Wickersham as the head of the National Commission on Law Observance and Enforcement, later popularly known as the Wickersham Commission.

Political cartoonists across the country satirized the commission's report to the President as a waste of taxpayers' money because the commissioners arrived at no new solutions to prohibition problems. So disgusted was the public by the government's failure to enforce the law consistently that by 1932 both political parties included the repeal of the 18th Amendment in their platform. The 21st Amendment was ratified in less than a year by the necessary three-fourths of the states. By 1933, national prohibition had ended.

Time: 1 or 1 1/2 class periods

Objectives:

• To briefly describe the activities of the Wickersham Commission.

• To identify and interpret the visual and written symbols within a political cartoon.

Materials Needed:

Document 60
Cartoon Analysis worksheet

Procedures:

1. Discuss the nature of symbols with your students. Ask students to develop a list of common American symbols frequently used by cartoonists. Your list might include Uncle Sam, John Q. Public, the Democratic donkey, and the Republican elephant.

2. Provide each student with copies of the cartoon and the Cartoon Analysis worksheet. You may wish to assign the first questions on the worksheet to individual students and to discuss the higher level questions with the class as a group.

3. We suggest you select one of the following assignments as a concluding activity for this exercise.

   a. Based on the information in the cartoon, write a paragraph describing the Wickersham Commission findings.

b. Collect several political cartoons and use the worksheet to analyze the elements of each cartoon.

c. Design a cartoon that illustrates your opinion on a specific issue of interest to you.

d. Compare and contrast a political cartoon with a comic strip. What are the differences in the symbols, characters, and messages of each?

Exercise 22
Crime: Its Causes in the 1920's

Note to the Teacher:

In this activity, students will investigate causes of crime in the 1920's and will examine seven letters to the National Commission on Law Observance and Enforcement for information to use in a role-playing activity. President Hoover established the commission in May 1929 in an effort to identify causes of criminal activity. Thousands of citizens wrote to George Wickersham, the commission's chairman, to offer information and to express opinions about the causes of crime in the United States. Examples of these letters are **documents 61-67**.

    Time: 1 class period

Objectives:

- To compare and contrast causes of crime between the 1920's and today.

- To participate effectively in role-playing and small group activities.

Materials Needed:

Documents 61-67

Procedures:

1. To motivate your students, write the following statement on the board: "The greatest cause of crime in the United States today is . . ."

    Ask students to complete this sentence. Discuss their responses and make a list of them on the board under the heading *Today*. Ask students to complete the same sentence as it might have been answered in the year 1925. Discuss and record student responses in a second list under the heading 1925. As a class, examine the two lists noting differences and similarities. Speculate on reasons for the differences. Keep both lists on the board during the remainder of this exercise.

2. Divide the class into groups of three or four students each and give each group one of the documents. Allow time for each group to read its document and to discuss the content.

3. Ask for a volunteer from each group to summarize the content of the document for other class members. Make a list on the board of the causes of crime mentioned in each document. Compare this list with the list of students' speculations about crime in 1925.

22

Direct students to consider:

a. What causes of crime were omitted from the 1925 list? Why?

b. What factors in your life today probably influenced your guesses about the causes of crime in 1925?

c. In addition to letters, what other sources of information would you consult to gain more information about crime in the 1920's?

d. In what ways have the causes of crime changed, if at all?

4. As an extended activity, direct students to write a paragraph beginning with one of the following topic sentences, followed by supporting information or arguments from the documents read in class.

The causes of crime in the United States *have not changed* since the 1920's.

OR

The causes of crime in the United States *have changed* significantly since the 1920's.

> 1309 Franklin St.,
>
> Johnstown, Pa.,
>
> Sept. 10, 1929.

The National Law Enforcement Commission,

Washington, D. C.

Gentlemen:

I understand that a committee has been appointed to study the cause of crime. This is very important indeed. For their consideration I beg to present a few things:

1. I enclose the front cover page of one copy of "Short Stories". I consider such pictures in our magazines and such stories which constantly tell of shooting *and other crimes* as a most prolific source of crime, for the young folks who see them and read them are inspired to do the same.

2. Moving Pictures *are* another source of crime. This has been proven again and again. For in many moving pictures crime is displayed and often the hero is guilty of crime himself, and so children are led to believe it is smart to commit a crime and often the proper thing to do.

These are two main causes of crime which could be largely eliminated by the following legislation:

All pictures of crime are prohibited on the screen, advertising posters, magazines and newspapers, etc.

All stories told so as to condone crime or praise it should be positively forbidden.

3. The ease with which people in America can buy firearms and ammunition is the <u>greatest</u> cause of crime in America. Why should every one indiscriminately be allowed to have a weapon?

I have lived for 25 years in India and with that large population we do not have as many crimes in a year as some of our cities

Exercise 23
Attitudes Toward Justice in the 1920's

Note to the Teacher:

This exercise focuses on newspaper editorials as sources of information. The two editorials document attitudes toward the administration of justice during the 1920's and provide an opportunity to discuss parallels with post Watergate attitudes on the subject.

Time: 1 class period

Objectives:

- To compare and contrast public attitudes toward justice between the 1920's and today.

- To compare and contrast newspapers with other types of primary sources.

- To identify an editorial's point of view.

Materials Needed:

Documents 68 and 69
Worksheet 15

Procedures:

1. Divide the class into two groups.

2. Provide several copies of one of the editorials to each group and a copy of the worksheet to each student.

3. The Shreveport *Times* editorial is more difficult to understand than that of the Cleveland *Press*. You may wish to review the vocabulary with students.

4. When the worksheets are complete, review them with students. Compare and contrast the points of view of the two editorials.

5. As a concluding discussion, consider one of these questions with your students:

    a. What do the editorials reveal about public attitudes toward justice in the 1920's? How reliable do you think they are as historical evidence?

    b. How do you think a historian might use these editorials?

    c. Do you think these editorials reflect current attitudes toward the administration of justice in the United States?

23

Exercise 23: Attitudes Toward Justice in the 1920's

Worksheet 15

Name of Newspaper:

Date of Newspaper:

1. What is the situation described in the editorial?

2. What is the editor's opinion about this situation?

3. What reasons does the editor offer for this opinion?

4. What is your reaction to the editorial? Do you agree or disagree with the editor's point of view? Why?

Exercise 24
Summary Exercise

Note to the Teacher:

In this exercise students will synthesize information about one aspect of the 1920's in a one-page paper. In addition to the unit documents and time line, you might encourage students to use their text and other secondary sources. You may wish to use this assignment as an extra credit project.

Time: open-ended

Objectives:

- To write a well-organized, one-page summary of life in the 1920's based on evidence in this teaching unit.

- To test a generalization.

Procedures:

1. Assign students to write one-page papers summarizing their impressions of life in America in the 1920's.

2. Make the documents, time line, and bibliography in this unit available to students and allow time for students to complete the assignment.

3. Direct students to select one of the following labels for the 1919-1929 decade and to defend its accuracy based on what they have learned from the documents and class activities.

    The Roaring 20's
    The Lawless Decade
    Wonderful Era of Nonsense
    The Age of Ballyhoo
    The Restless Decade
    The Fabulous Decade
    Turbulent Twenties
    Teeming Twenties
    The Jazz Age

4. Students should begin their papers with a topic sentence stating their choice and then substantiate that choice with facts from the documents and other materials used in their study of the 1920's.

5. When the papers are complete, ask students to discuss the reasons they selected the label they did.

Time Line

This time line is not meant to be comprehensive; in fact, we have included some entries about the lighter side of the decade. You may refer your students to the time line to aid them in relating specific events or incidents described in the documents to other national events.

1920 **January 1 & 2** U.S. Attorney General A. Mitchell Palmer conducts the two largest government raids against suspected communists and anarchists, arresting several thousand. These massive arrests cause a public outcry resulting in the end to the raids by May.

January 16 The 18th Amendment (prohibition) - outlawing the manufacture, sale, and transport of alcoholic beverages - becomes law.

May 31 The first trial of Nicola Sacco and Bartolomeo Vanzetti, Italian anarchists accused of killing a paymaster and guard in South Braintree, MA. They are found guilty on July 14, 1920, but their case is appealed and drags on for most of the decade.

August 26 The 19th Amendment, granting equal voting rights for women, takes effect.

September 16 A bomb, apparently intended to kill wealthy capitalists like J. P. Morgan, explodes on Wall Street. Ironically, the only people killed are passers-by and clerks in nearby buildings.

October 12 Construction begins on the Holland Tunnel, connecting New York City with New Jersey for automobile traffic.

1921 **March 4** Warren G. Harding is inaugurated 29th President of the United States.

July 2 The United States makes a separate peace with Germany, formally ending the hostilities of World War I. The U.S. Senate had failed to ratify the Versailles Treaty to avoid U.S. involvement in the League of Nations.

September 8 First beauty pageant in Atlantic City, NJ. The ban on bare knees and skintight bathing suits is temporarily suspended. This event, won by Margaret Gorman, helps to popularize the one-piece bathing suit.

November 11 The Unknown Soldier is buried as a memorial to all U.S. soldiers who had died in World War I and were neither identified nor found. Heads of state from Italy, Germany, Japan, France, and Great Britain, among others, participate in this event.

November 12 The Washington Conference on Naval Limitation limits the size of the navies of the United States, Great Britain, Japan, France, and Italy.

December 25 Socialist leader Eugene V. Debs, jailed under the wartime Espionage Act, is pardoned by President Harding and released from prison.

1922 **September 16** The murdered bodies of Reverend Hall and a choir singer, Mrs. Mills, are discovered. Reverend Hall's wife and her two brothers are charged with the murders, tried, and later found innocent.

November 4 Howard Carter, on an expedition funded by Lord Carnarvon of England, discovers the tomb of King Tut-Ankh-Amen in the Valley of the Tombs of the Kings in Egypt.

1923 **March 30 & 31** Alma Cummings becomes the first dance marathon champion by dancing 27 straight hours, exhausting her six partners.

April 18 Yankee Stadium opens in the Bronx, NY.

May 21 Nathan Leopold and Richard Loeb murder Bobby Franks. Clarence Darrow later defends the accused. While admitting their guilt, Darrow puts the human brain "on trial" by arguing that the two boys were mentally ill. Leopold and Loeb each receive prison terms for the murder and kidnapping, but Darrow's arguments save them from the death penalty.

	August 2	President Warren G. Harding dies in San Francisco, CA.
	August 3	Vice President Calvin Coolidge is sworn in as President by his father, a notary public, in the family farmhouse in Plymouth, VT.
	August 13	"Yes, We Have No Bananas" becomes the #1 hit song.
	December 31	The first vocal transatlantic radio broadcast is transmitted.
1924	February 3	Former President Woodrow Wilson dies.
	May 15	Congress passes a new quota law for immigration. This law sets immigration quotas that effectively exclude Asians and most southeastern Europeans.
	June 2	Congress grants American Indians full U.S. citizenship in response to their service in World War I. Previously, Indians were not regarded as citizens, but as wards of the federal government.
	June 30	Former Secretary of Interior Albert B. Fall is indicted on charges of fraud and corruption in a scandal involving the lease of government naval oil reserve lands to private investors. This indictment is part of a scandal that becomes known as Teapot Dome.
	July 1	Regular airmail service starts between San Francisco, CA, and New York, N.Y.
	November 4	Calvin Coolidge is elected 30th President of the United States, defeating John Davis, Democrat, and Robert LaFollette, Progressive. Coolidge's campaign slogans were "Keep Cool with Coolidge," and "Coolidge Prosperity."
1925	January 8	With the swearing in of three women - Hortense Ward, Hattie Henenberg, and Ruth Brazzil - to the Texas State Supreme Court, that court becomes the first all-woman state supreme court.
	January 24	A total eclipse of the sun catches the attention of many Americans.
	July 10-21	The trial of John Scopes in Dayton, TN. The press represents this trial as a conflict between religious fundamentalism and liberal science. Scopes, a biology teacher, is being tried for teaching the theory of evolution in school (an earlier Tennessee law forbade teaching this theory). The American Civil Liberties Union retains Clarence Darrow as Scopes' lawyer, while William Jennings Bryan prosecutes the case for the state. While Scopes is convicted, the publicity of the case limits the spread of similar state laws.
	July 26	William Jennings Bryan, three-time presidential candidate and former Secretary of State, dies in Dayton, TN. Many view this as the passing of one of America's greatest men.
	October 31	Henry Ford's automobile factory achieves the record of producing one car every 10 seconds.
1926	January 7	The first commercial transatlantic telephone service is established between New York City and London.
	May 9	Adm. Richard Byrd and his companion, Floyd Bennett, become the first men to fly over the North Pole.
	May 18	Aimee Semple McPherson, a west coast popular revivalist, disappears, reportedly kidnapped and killed. She reappears on June 23. Later investigations reveal that she had run off with a radio operator from her "Temple."
	June 1	The first electric toaster is marketed.
	July 17	The Hall-Mills murder case is reopened with new evidence. (See Sept. 16, 1922, entry.) The jury still finds the accused, Mrs. Hall and her two brothers, innocent.
	August 6	A young German-American, Gertrude (Trudy) Ederle, is the first woman to swim the English Channel. By swimming the 35-mile channel in 14 hours and 31 seconds, she sets a new time record.

August 23	Actor Rudolph Valentino dies of complications from an appendectomy in New York City. Huge crowds line up outside the funeral home for 3 hours for a 2-second glimpse of the star's body. The crowd shatters the funeral home windows and tears up much of Lincoln Square.
September 23	The first Tunney-Dempsey boxing match. "Gentleman" Gene Tunney defeats the titleholder, Jack Dempsey.
1927 May 20	Charles A. Lindbergh, Jr., leaves Roosevelt Field in New York City for his transatlantic flight to Paris, France. Unlike his competitors, Lindbergh flies alone. After a flight of 33 1/2 hours, Lindbergh arrives in Paris on May 22. He is wildly cheered in Paris and later is welcomed home with the largest tickertape parade in New York City history.
May 26	The Supreme Court rules that bootleggers must file income tax statements on income from their illegal activities. They cannot plead self-incrimination as an excuse for failing to report their income.
August 23	Sacco and Vanzetti, despite many protests, die in the electric chair in the Charlestown State Prison in Massachusetts. (See May 31, 1920, entry.)
September 22	The Dempsey-Tunney rematch fight goes down in boxing history as the Fight of the Long Count. (When Tunney went down, it was claimed that he was given 13 seconds, not the regulation 10, to recover.) Tunney goes on to win the fight, but many consider his win unfair.
September 30	Babe Ruth hits his 60th home run, superseding his own home run record of 59 in one season.
October 6	The movie *The Jazz Singer*, starring Al Jolson, is released. This is the first all-sound movie with the human voice talking and singing.
December 2	Henry Ford introduces his Model A to replace the popular Model T. The Model A is available in four colors, while the Model T was "any color you want, as long as it is black."
1928 August 27	The United States and 14 other nations sign the Kellogg-Briand Pact. The pact supersedes the Washington Conference Treaty and calls on all signers to renounce war except as a defensive measure.
September 19	Cartoonist Walt Disney introduces Mickey Mouse to movie audiences in *Steamboat Willie*.
November 6	Herbert Hoover is elected 31st President of the United States, defeating Al Smith, Democrat.
1929 January 15	Martin Luther King, Jr., future civil rights leader, is born.
February 14	The St. Valentine's Day Massacre in Chicago, IL. Members of Al Capone's gang surprise and murder seven members of the rival Bugs Moran gang. The murderers are never apprehended.
October 24	Black Thursday. The stock market takes its largest dip of the year but is bolstered up by a group of bankers. The market closes early on Friday and Saturday. On Monday, October 28, the market seems to be recovering.
October 29	Black Tuesday. The stock market takes a sudden plunge down; investors panic and start selling, hoping to get out before losing everything.
November 8	Adm. Richard Byrd flies over the South Pole.

Annotated Bibliography

General History

Allen, Frederick Lewis. *Only Yesterday: An Informal History of the 1920's*. New York: Bonanza Books: distributed by Crown Publishers, 1986.

>Writing shortly after the close of the 1920's, Allen explores trends in the attitudes of society during the 1920's. He shows the public's reaction to major figures and events. Allen skillfully ties the Big Bull Market and consequent stock market crash to the speculating fever of the 1920's. The reader should be cautious, however, in accepting Allen's final conclusions since he wrote the book before the end of the Great Depression. Recommended for students and teachers.

Allsop, Kenneth. *The Bootleggers*. New Rochelle, NY: Arlington House, Inc., 1961.

>This is a history of the growth of the bootlegging industry and gangsterism during the 1920's. Allsop covers the ins and outs of gang warfare and its effects on society. He also discusses the government's inability to understand and control the closed society of the immigrant/ gangster's world. Recommended for teachers and advanced students.

Boardman, Fon W., Jr. *America and the Jazz Age*. New York: Henry Z. Walck, Inc., Publishers, 1968.

>This book is written in a simple flowing style, making it interesting and easy to read. Boardman examines political and social trends and public attitudes of the 1920's. Recommended for students.

Davis, Ronald L., ed. *The Social and Cultural Life of the 1920's*. New York: Holt, Rinehart and Winston, Inc., 1972.

>This book is a collection of essays and excerpts from books on the social life of the 1920's. The essays are grouped by themes, such as "The Search for Meaning and Individualism" and "Literature and the Arts." The essays are well written, in depth, and very revealing of the 1920's. Recommended for students and teachers.

Dumenil, Lynn. *The Modern Temper: American Culture and Society in the 1920s*. New York: Hill and Wang, 1995.

>Dumenil's fascinating look at American society in the 1920s reveals the inherent stresses and tensions of the decades that are often overlooked by those hoping to mythologize the "Roaring Twenties." Suggested for teachers.

Goldberg, David Joseph. *Discontented America: The United States in the 1920s*. Baltimore: Johns Hopkins University Press, 1999.

>A well executed attempt to debunk the glamor of the "Roaring Twenties," this work situates the 1920s as a distinctly postwar decade, when many of the issues raised for American society during World War I remained unresolved. Suggested for teachers.

Leuchtenburg, William E. *The Perils of Prosperity, 1914-1932*. 2d ed. Chicago: University of Chicago Press, 1993.

>Leuchtenburg offers an unusual viewpoint toward the 1920's. He does not discuss major events or major persons in the typical way. He examines the social attitudes of classes, such as the literati and the rural farmers. Leuchtenburg shows how activities and attitudes of the 1920's laid the foundations not only for the Great Depression but also for World War II. Recommended for teachers and advanced students.

*Parrish, Michael E. *Anxious Decades: America in Prosperity and Depression, 1920-1941.* New York: W.W. Norton, 1992.

> A broad work of political, social, and economic American history during the roaring twenties and the Great Depression, this book provides a general overview of the United States during this period. The work includes a hefty bibliographic chapter with suggestions for further reading. Recommended for both students and teachers.

Sann, Paul. *The Lawless Decade.* New York: Da Capo Press, 1984.

> This book is a pictorial-textual history of the 1920's. Sann deals with important themes of the decade, such as prohibition and the Ku Klux Klan. He provides photos and a written text to illustrate the social and/or political happenings. The book is arranged by year, highlighting the most significant events with a brief synopsis of other events. Attractively illustrated, Sann's book is a popular account of the 1920's but uneven in its historical reliability. Recommended for students and teachers.

*Shaw, Arnold. *The Jazz Age: Popular Music in the 1920s.* New York: Oxford University Press, 1987.

> Shaw's investigation of the impact of the Jazz Age captures the spirit of the era, discusses how jazz influenced and in turn was influenced by American culture during the roaring twenties, and explains how it continued to influence American music well into the 1950s. The book includes a discography for reference, as well as a detailed bibliography with suggestions for further reading. Suggested for students and teachers.

Sullivan, Mark. *Our Times.* New York: Scribner, 1996.

> This abridged version of Sullivan's six-volume set of American history discusses the years 1900-25. Volume VI discusses the 1920's. Sullivan discusses Harding and his political career, then moves on to literary, musical, and theatrical changes that took place. This book is interesting because it is based on interviews with important people of the decade, and Sullivan catches the humor and carefree attitudes of that time. Recommended for students and teachers.

Werstein, Irving. *Shattered Decade, 1919-1929.* New York: Charles Scribner's Sons, 1970.

> This is a colorful history of the 1920's. Werstein touches on some of the decade's major movements and events in America. He also covers major events in Europe and their impact on America. Recommended for students.

Autobiographies

Byrd, Richard E. *Little America.* New York: G. P. Putnam's Sons, 1930.

> This is Byrd's personal account of his South Pole expedition with all its triumphs and problems. He gives details of what he saw, what he experienced, and the men who were with him. Recommended for students.

Hoover, Herbert. *On Growing Up.* New York: William Morrow & Co., Inc. 1962.

> This small volume is a collection of letters written to President Herbert Hoover by young children and his responses to the letters. The letters give insight into the concerns of children while revealing an unseen side of President Hoover. Recommended for students.

Lindbergh, Charles A., Jr. *We*. New York: G. P. Putnam's Sons, 1927.

> In Lindbergh's personal account of his famous flight, he talks of the months of preparation and the flight itself, revealing his feelings and thoughts. Recommended for students.

Rogers, Will. *Ether and Me*. Stillwater: Oklahoma State University Press, 1973.

> This is Will Rogers' version of his gallbladder operation. The book is very short and amusing, offering real insight into the man and his personality. Recommended for students.

White, Walter. *A Man Called White*. Athens: University of Georgia Press, 1995.

> White was one of the first executive directors and executive secretaries of the National Association for the Advancement of Colored People (NAACP). His life story reveals the social conditions of the South in the 1920's and the prejudices toward blacks. Recommended for students.

Biographies

Adams, Samuel Hopkins. *Incredible Era*. New York: Octagon Books, 1979.

> In this biography of President Harding, Adams focuses on Harding's unwillingness to be President, his inability to pick good advisers, and his failures and successes as President. Recommended for teachers and advanced students.

Berg, A. Scott. *Lindbergh*. New York: G. P. Putnam's, 1998.

> A comprehensive look at the controversial life of aviator Charles Lindberg, Berg's book captures the spirit of not only Lindberg the man but also the times in which he lived, particularly the 1920s, when Lindberg became the most famous man in the world literally overnight. Well written and easy to read, this biography is suggested for both teachers and students.

Cavanah, Frances. *Meet the Presidents*. Philadelphia: Macrae Smith Company, 1964.

> This volume contains short essays on all the Presidents. The three essays on the Presidents of the 1920's chronicle episodes from their childhood and incidents from their years as President. Recommended for students.

Greenfield, Howard. *F. Scott Fitzgerald*. New York: Crown Publishers, Inc., 1974.

> This is an easily readable biography of Fitzgerald. It tells of his difficulty in handling success and the tragic end of his marriage and his life. Recommended for students.

Ketchum, Richard M. *Will Rogers, His Life and Times*. New York: American Heritage Publishing Co., Inc., 1973.

> Refreshing and humorous, this book looks at the 1920's (and early 1930's) through the eyes of America's beloved humorist Will Rogers. The emphasis is on Will Rogers' role as ambassador of good will, his activities in events of national importance, and his contacts with average people. Included are a number of photographs. Recommended for students.

Letts, Mary. *Al Capone*. New York: St. Martin's Press, 1975.

> This short biography of Al Capone discusses his life from his early childhood to his downfall in the 1930's. The book is written in a simple style. Recommended for students.

Lyons, Eugene. *Herbert Hoover*. Norwalk, CT: Easton Press, 1989.

> In this detailed biography of President Hoover, Lyons analyzes Hoover's insight into post-World War I European affairs and the need for United States aid. Lyons also is concerned with Hoover's presidency and his attempts to keep the American people afloat in the early years of the Depression. Recommended for teachers.

Lyons, Eugene. *Our Unknown Ex-President*. Washington: Human Events, 1959.

> This informal history of Herbert Hoover covers his childhood, his rise to wealth, his successes in Europe, and his attempts to turn the tide of the Depression. Recommended for students.

Maglangbayan, Shawna. *Garvey, Lumumba, Malcolm: Black National-Separatists*. Chicago: Third World Press, 1972.

> This book contains brief biographies of three black American separatists. One essay is on Marcus Garvey, who helped many blacks find self-pride in the 1920's. Maglangbayan's analysis takes a new look at Garvey and his life work; it is a fresh perspective through the eyes of a black author. Recommended for students.

Mosley, Leonard. *Lindbergh, A Biography*. Mineola, NY: Dover Publications, 2000.

> In this detailed biography of Lindbergh, Mosley reveals the joys and pains the Lindbergh family experienced during their lives. He also focuses on their attempts to avoid the press and their abhorrence of fame. Mosley shows the human side of the great hero and his family. Recommended for students and teachers.

Richardson, Ben, and Fahey, William. *Great Black Americans*. New York: Thomas Y. Crowell Company, Inc., 1976.

> This book is a series of short biographical essays on black Americans in the fields of music, science, and literature, such as Louis Armstrong, Langston Hughes, and George Washington Carver. Recommended for students.

Ross, Walter. *The Last Hero*. New York: Harper & Row, 1976.

> Written while Lindbergh was still alive, this biography is easily readable. It covers Lindbergh's life from his childhood through the lives of his children. Recommended for students.

Speiring, Frank. *The Man Who Got Capone*. New York: The Bobbs Merrill Co., Inc., 1976.

> This is a biography of Treasury Agent Frank Wilson, whose efforts culminated in the trial and conviction of Al Capone. The book is a study of Wilson's investigation and the trial of Al Capone. Recommended for students.

Prohibition

Barry, James P. *The Noble Experiment*. New York: Franklin Watts, Inc., 1972.

> Written in a simple style, this book tells the story of prohibition. Barry details the origins of the prohibition movement and its social consequences. Recommended for students.

Chidsey, Donald Barr. *On and Off the Wagon*. New York: Cowles Book Co., 1969.

> This book is an amusing study of the prohibition movement in the United States. Beginning in chapter 14, he treats the 1920's and the various successes and failures of the prohibition amendment. Recommended for students.

Sacco and Vanzetti Case

Frankfurter, Felix. *The Case of Sacco and Vanzetti*. New York, Universal Library 1962.

> Written for laymen, this little volume is a lawyer's review of the evidence and trial of Nicola Sacco and Bartolomeo Vanzetti. The analysis is detailed, but Frankfurter offers no conclusions in the case. Recommended for students and teachers.

Russell, Francis. *Tragedy in Dedham*. New York: McGraw-Hill Book Company, 1971.

> This is an in depth analysis of the Sacco-Vanzetti case. Russell concludes that Sacco was guilty, Vanzetti was not. His reasons are interesting, but the book raises anew the questions of the case and the evidence. Recommended for teachers and advanced students.

Women in the 1920's

Clark, Electa. *Leading Ladies*. New York: Stein and Day, 1976.

> Chapter III of this book pertains to women in the 1920's. In this chapter, Clark examines the changing attitudes of many women toward the feminist movement in the 1920's. She also discusses the reactions of older feminists to these changing attitudes. Clark then gives short biographies of various famous women of the 1920's. Recommended for students.

Latham, Angela J. *Posing a Threat: Flappers, Chorus Girls, and Other Brazen Performers of the American 1920s.* Hanover, NH: Wesleyan University Press, 2000.

> Using women's fashion as a springboard, this book re-examines the role of women in American society in the 1920s. Latham's work is written for other scholars and relies on academia's predominant gender theory but includes many interesting dicussions of changing perceptions regarding women and women's rising profile in such American cultural pursuits as beauty pageants and stage productions. Suggested for teachers only.

Showalter, Elaine, ed. *These Modern Women*. Old Westbury, NY: The Feminist Press, 1989.

> This book is a series of essays, written by women in the 1920's. The women tell what factors in their lives they believe influenced their choices of independence and feminism. Included are three essays by psychologists, analyzing the women's essays and the essays' reflection of women's changing attitudes. Recommended for students or teachers.

Sochen, June. *Movers and Shakers*. New York: Quadrangle/The N.Y. Times Bk. Co., 1973.

> This book is a review of the feminist movement from 1900 to 1970. Chapter III treats the period 1920-40. The book is well written and interesting. Recommended for students.

The 1920's

Archival Citations of Documents

1. Maxwell Car ad, *The Literary Digest*, April 11, 1925; File 9: 2 Ads for cars-Oldsmobile Six Maxwell; DJ Central Files; 23-0-2 to 23-0-2; General Records of the Department of Justice, Record Group 60; National Archives at College Park, College Park, MD.

2. Cartoon, Chicago *Daily Tribune*, August 23, 1924; Political cartoon from Chicago *Daily Tribune*; Teapot Dome Files: 226016, section 1; General Records of the Department of Justice, Record Group 60; National Archives at College Park, College Park, MD.

3. "Girl, Boy, Bottle…," Elizabethton *Star* (TN), April 18, 1929; The Elizabethton *Star*, 4/18/29;280; 170/ 4904; Textile, Gastonia, NC, Pictures, Press; Records of the Federal Mediation and Conciliation Service, Record Group 280; National Archives at College Park, College Park, MD.

4. Report of metropolitan police department, *17th Annual Reports of Departments*, 1922, Vincennes, Indiana.; Vincennes, Indiana; *Seventeenth Annual Report* Pamphlet; Records of the U.S. Coal Commission, Record Group 68; National Archives at College Park, College Park, MD.

5. Photograph No. 33-SC-4849; Hood River County, Oregon, July 20, 1925; Records of the Federal Extension Service, Record Group 33; National Archives at College Park, College Park, MD.

6. Letter to George W. Wickersham from a mother, July 22, 1929; General Records, General Correspondence; Office of the Chairman; Records of the National Commission on Law Observance and Enforcement, Record Group 10; National Archives at College Park, College Park, MD.

7. Telegram to Thomas R. Marshall from John R. Shillady, Secretary, NAACP, Cleveland, OH, June 26, 1919; Senate Judiciary Committee; Anti-Lynching Laws (SEN66A-F12); 66th Congress; Records of the U.S. Senate, Record Group 46; National Archives Building, Washington, DC.

8. Graph of trend of prices and purchasing power, n.d.; Chart of farm costs/profits, 1913-22;(BAE Source); Agricultural Situation; Incoming Correspondence; Records of the Office of the Secretary of Agriculture, Record Group 16; National Archives at College Park, College Park, MD.

9. Letter to the Hon. Philander C. Knox from R.A. Craford, U.M.W. District 2, December 9, 1920; "Various Subjects"; Resolution of U.M.W. Local No. 3519, Bennington, PA; (SEN66-J40); 66th Congress; Records of the U.S. Senate, Record Group 46; National Archives Building, Washington, DC.

10. Letter to Henry A. Wallace from Albert O. Fisher, August 15, 1923; Agricultural Situation; General Correspondence; Records of the Office of the Secretary of Agriculture, Record Group 16; National Archives at College Park, College Park, MD.

11. Editorial, *Wall Street Journal*, September 27, 1921; Editorial regarding boll weevil: Attached to letter 9/27/21; Agricultural Situation; General Correspondence; Records of the Office of the Secretary of Agriculture, Record Group 16; National Archives at College Park, College Park, MD.

12. Letter to Bradford Knapp from T.O. Walton, December 31, 1918; Negro File, 1909-1923, (1919 Folder); General Correspondence; Records of the Office of the Secretary of Agriculture, Record Group 16; National Archives at College Park, College Park, MD.

13. "Says the Foreigner is not Appreciated," Brooklyn *Standard Union*, March 23, 1921; 219; Aliens, Ellis Island Immigration Station; Central File (1897 - 1923); Box 38/219 (1918-23); Records of the Public Health Service, Record Group 90; National Archives at College Park, College Park, MD.

14. Letter to the Hon. Secretary of Labor, Washington, DC, from F.A. Canizares, September 20, 1922; 164/14C, Letter from R.H. Johnson Co., 9/20/1922; Chief Clerk's Files, 164/14-164/14D; General Records, 1907- 1942; Records of the Department of Labor, Record Group 174; National Archives at College Park, College Park, MD.

15. Letter to U.S. Senate from Loggia Beatrice Cenci No. 1207, February 9, 1924; (SEN68A-J27); 68th Congress; Records of the United States Senate, Record Group 46; National Archives Building, Washington, DC.

16. Letter to President Calvin Coolidge from Alliance Klan #1, May 15, 1924; 164/14,To Calvin Coolidge, 5/15/24, from women of KKK; Chief Clerk's Files, 164/14-164/14D; General Records, 1907-1942; Records of the Department of Labor, Record Group 174; National Archives at College Park, College Park, MD.

17. Photograph No. 90-G-885; "Ellis Island, NY," 1923; Records of the Public Health Service, Record Group 90; National Archives at College Park, College Park, MD.

18. Letter to the Hon. Woodrow Wilson from George A. Murray, February 14, 1920; P-19-3, to Woodrow Wilson from George Murray, 2/14/20, regarding separate facilities; Records of the U.S. Railroad Administration, Record Group 14; National Archives at College Park, College Park, MD.

19. Letter to the Hon. Henry C. Wallace from H.L. Remmel, October 3, 1923; Negro File, 1909-1923; General Correspondence, 1923; Records of the Office of the Secretary of Agriculture, Record Group 16; National Archives at College Park, College Park, MD.

20. Letter to the Hon. Third Assistant, Division of Classification [U.S. Post Office Department], from H.C. Blalock, July 17, 1919; B349, Marshall, Texas, 4/17/1919; Records of the U.S. Postal Service, Record Group 28; National Archives Building, Washington, DC.

21. Memorandum for Walker D. Hines from Max Thelen, June 21, 1919; P19-3; Records of the U.S. Railroad Administration, Record Group 14; National Archives at College Park, College Park, MD.

22. Ad, The Chicago *Defender*, September 27, 1919; B349; Records of the U.S. Postal Service, Record Group 28; National Archives Building, Washington, DC.

23. Flyer from the NAACP, n.d.; Judiciary Committee; Investigation of Race Riots, Lynchings, 8x10 poster, "3000 Negroes will burn"; (SEN66A-F12); 66th Congress; Records of the U.S. Senate, Record Group 46; National Archives Building, Washington, DC.

24. Letter to the Department of Justice from Mrs. H. Lipsett, April 19, 1929; DJ Central Files; Straight Numerical Files: 202-600; General Section 5; General Records of the Department of Justice, Record Group 60; National Archives at College Park, College Park, MD

25. Letter to Walker D. Hines from M.W. Briggs, September 19, 1919; File P19-3; Complaints about Negroes on high class trains; Records of the U.S. Railroad Administration, Record Group 14; National Archives at College Park, College Park, MD.

26. Letter to Warren G. Harding from Ara Lee Settle, June 18, 1922; DJ Central Files; Straight Numerical Files: 158260, Sub 141-232; General Records of the Department of Justice, Record Group 60; National Archives at College Park, College Park, MD.

27. Letter to Mrs. Mable Walker Willebrandt from Gladys W. Center, November 21, 1928; DJ Central Files; Classified Subject Files (23-0-15); General Records of the Department of Justice, Record Group 60; National Archives at College Park, College Park, MD.

28. Letter to President Herbert Hoover from Horace Robinson, November 20, 1929; DJ Central Files; Straight Numerical Files: 158-260, Sub 233; General Records of the Department of Justice, Record Group 60; National Archives at College Park, College Park, MD.

29. Survey of Pathfinders of America, ca. 1924; File O, attachment to letter to O.H. Blackman from Grace Abbott; Records of the Children's Bureau, Record Group 102; National Archives at College Park, College Park, MD.

30. Letter to the Hon. Calvin Coolidge from Charles D. Levy, June 24, 1924; DJ Central Files; Straight Numerical: 198589, Sub 560-619 (5); General Records of the Department of Justice, Record Group 60; National Archives at College Park, College Park, MD.

31. Flyer, "The Ku Klux Klan Invites You to the Portals...," n.d.; Flyer promoting the KKK, Baltimore, MD; DJ Central Files; Straight Numerical Files:198-589, Sub 440-499; General Records of the Department of Justice, Record Group 60; National Archives at College Park, College Park, MD.

32. Letter to Warren G. Harding from Arthur James Mann, September 24, 1921; DJ Central Files; Straight Numerical Files: 198-589; General Records of the Department of Justice, Record Group 60; National Archives at College Park, College Park, MD.

33. Photograph No. 306-NT-650-4; "KKK women marching, Washington, DC," 1928; Records of the International Communication Agency, Record Group 306; National Archives at College Park, College Park, MD.

34. Letter to Attorney General John G. Sargeant from Rampy J. Burdick, March 3, 1928; DJ Central Files; Straight Numerical Files: 198-589; General Records of the Department of Justice, Record Group 60; National Archives at College Park, College Park, MD.

35. Photograph No. 306-NT-10506C; "President Calvin Coolidge," n.d.; Records of the International Communication Agency, Record Group 306; National Archives at College Park, College Park, MD.

36. Letter to Hon. Calvin Coolidge from W.E. Ryan, July 28, 1924; DJ Central Files; Straight Numerical Files: 198-589, Sub 560-619(5); General Records of the Department of Justice, Record Group 60; National Archives at College Park, College Park, MD.

37. Letter to Department of Justice from Isaac McClellan, February 10, 1923; DJ Central Files; Straight Numerical Files: 198-589, Sub 560-619(5); General Records of the Department of Justice, Record Group 60; National Archives at College Park, College Park, MD.

38. Letter to U.S. District Attorney Harlan F. Stone from S. Jonce, December 5, 1924; DJ Central Files; Straight Numerical Files: 198-589, Sub 560-619(5); General Records of the Department of Justice, Record Group 60; National Archives at College Park, College Park, MD.

39. Photograph No. 28-MS-3A-11; "Charles A. Lindbergh loading cargo, Lambert Field, St. Louis," 1925; American Image #221; Records of the U.S. Postal Service, Record Group 28; National Archives at College Park, College Park, MD.

40. Post Office Department map of airmail routes, April 24, 1926; United States Air Mail Routes, 1926; Records of the U.S. Postal Service, Record Group 28; National Archives at College Park, College Park, MD.

41. Post Office Department map of airmail routes, August 1, 1928; United States Air Mail Routes, 1928; Records of the U.S. Postal Service, Record Group 28; National Archives at College Park, College Park, MD.

42. Advertisement for laundry supplies, Montgomery Ward catalog, 1922-23; Investigation File: House Furnishings; Com. 6, Mon 5, W5/Montgomery Ward; "Laundry Supplies Page"; Economic Division; Records of the Federal Trade Commission, Record Group 122; National Archives at College Park, College Park, MD.

43. Advertisement for the 1900 Cataract Washer, n.d.; Investigative File: House Furnishings; Com. 6, Nin 5, B5/Nineteen Hundred Washer Co.; Economic Division; Records of the Federal Trade Commission, Record Group 122; National Archives at College Park, College Park, MD.

44. Advertisement from Danciger Brumalt Co., n.d.; File 2: 23-0-1-1-23-2: Brumalt-"make it yourself"; General Records of the Department of Justice, Record Group 60; National Archives at College Park, College Park, MD.

45. Letter to Hon George P. McLean from Legislative Committee, Connecticut Council of Catholic Women, February 4, 1924; (SEN68A-J35); 68th Congress; Records of the U.S. Senate, Record Group 46; National Archives Building, Washington, DC.

46. House Joint Resolution 75, 68th Congress, lst session; Committee on the Judiciary; (HR68A-D18); 68th Congress; Records of the U.S. House of Representatives, Record Group 233; National Archives Building, Washington, DC.

47. Charts relating to the employment of men and women, *Statistical Atlas of the United States*, 1924, p. 256 and 267; Records of the Bureau of the Census, Record Group 29; National Archives at College Park, College Park, MD.

48. Photograph No. NWDNS-86-G-10F(15); "Telephone operators," April 7, 1927; Records of the Women's Bureau, Record Group 86; National Archives at College Park, College Park, MD.

49. Suggested window display from *Help for the Dealer*, Landers, Frary and Clark, New Britain, CT, n.d.; Investigative File: House Furnishings; Com 6, Lan 5, B5/Landers, Frary, and Clark; Economic Division; Records of the Federal Trade Commission, Record Group 122; National Archives at College Park, College Park, MD.

50. Letter to the Hon. James A. Davis from J.O. Wells, April 20, 1923; 164/14D; Chief Clerk's Files, 164/14-164/14D; General Records, 1907-1942; Records of the Department of Labor, Record Group 174; National Archives at College Park, College Park, MD.

51. Newspaper page, the Omaha *World Herald*, November 24, 1929; "Stranded in New York"; Editorials and Cartoons; Office of the Secretary, To the Chairman, Letters from the Public; Records of the National Commission on Law Observance and Enforcement, Record Group 10; National Archives at College Park, College Park, MD.

52. Photograph No. 306-VT-170-365C; "Still," n.d.; Records of the International Communication Agency, Record Group 306; National Archives at College Park, College Park, MD.

53. Unidentified editorial, 1929; Editorials and Cartoons; Office of the Secretary, To the Chairman, Letters from the Public; Records of the National Commission on Law Observance and Enforcement, Record Group 10; National Archives at College Park, College Park, MD.

54. Resolution to the Hon. Calvin Coolidge from the City Council of Baltimore concerning prohibition, January 24, 1922; Records of the U.S. Senate, Record Group 46; National Archives Building, Washington, DC.

55. Letter to Mr. G.W. Wickersham from a Citizen of Arkansas, July 17, 1929; Letter with Hotel Chisca letterhead, July 17, 1929; General Records, General Correspondence; Office of the Chairman; Records of the National Commission on Law Observance and Enforcement, Record Group 10; National Archives at College Park, College Park, MD.

56. Letter to the Hon. Frank B. Kellogg from Mrs. W.C. Hair, January 6, 1926; File 811.114.4478; Central Decimal Files, 1910-1929; General Records of the Department of State, Record Group 59; National Archives at College Park, College Park, MD.

57. Letter to Miss Mabel Willebrant [sic] from O.A. Calandria, n.d.; Received 4/30/29; DJ Central Files; Classified Subject Files: 23-0-19; General Records of the Department of Justice, Record Group 60; National Archives at College Park, College Park, MD.

58. Newspaper article, *Appleton Post-Crescent*, n.d.; Doc A; DJ Central Files; Classified Subject Files: 23-0-13; General Records of the Department of Justice, Record Group 60; National Archives at College Park, College Park, MD.

59. Letter to Henry C. Wallace from J.O. Robertson, August 14, 1922; Incoming Correspondence; Records of the Office of the Secretary of Agriculture, Record Group 16; National Archives at College Park, College Park, MD.

60. Cartoon, Columbus *Dispatch*, January 21, 1931; Cartoons, "Prohibition Cartoons"; Cartoon-*Dispatch*-Columbus, Ohio; Editorials and Cartoons, (2B-D8), 1930-31; Office of the Secretary, To the Chairman, Letters from the Public; Records of the National Commission on Law Observance and Enforcement, Record Group 10; National Archives at College Park, College Park, MD.

61. Letter to President Herbert Hoover from Alva P. Jones, May 25, 1929; Letter to H. Hoover from National Cigarette Law Enforcement League, 5/25/29; "J", 1929; Office of the Chairman, General Records, General Correspondence; Records of the National Commission on Law Observance and Enforcement, Record Group 10; National Archives at College Park, College Park, MD.

62. Letter to the National Law Enforcement Commission from J.M. Blough, September 10, 1929, with attachment; "B", 1929; Office of the Chairman, General Records, General Correspondence; Records of the National Commission on Law Observance and Enforcement, Record Group 10; National Archives at College Park, College Park, MD.

63. Letter to the Hon. George W. Wickersham from A.B. Geary, June 6, 1929; "G", 1929; Office of the Chairman, General Records, General Correspondence; Records of the National Commission on Law Observance and Enforcement, Records Group 10; National Archives at College Park, College Park, MD.

64. Letter to the Hon. George W. Wickersham from George W. Dexter, June 10, 1929; Role of Press in Crime; "D", 1929; Office of the Chairman, General Records, General Correspondence; Records of the National Commission on Law Observance and Enforcement, Record Group 10; National Archives at College Park, College Park, MD.

65. Letter to George W. Wickersham from William T. Elzinga, June 16, 1929; "E", 1929; Office of the Chairman, General Records, General Correspondence; Records of the National Commission on Law Observance and Enforcement, Record Group 10; National Archives at College Park, College Park, MD.

66. Letter to the President from Arthur R. Boyden, August 5, 1929; Hollywood, CA; "B", 1929; Office of the Chairman, General Records, General Correspondence; Records of the National Commission on Law Observance and Enforcement, Record Group 10; National Archives at College Park, College Park, MD.

67. Letter to Crime and Law Enforcement [Commission] from John E. Ayor, M.V., May 23, 1929; Letter-New England Club heading; "A", 1929; Office of the Chairman, General Records, General Correspondence; Records of the National Commission on Law Observance and Enforcement, Record Group 10; National Archives at College Park, College Park, MD.

68. Editorial, *The Shreveport Times*, May 5, 1929; Editorials and Cartoons; Office of the Secretary, To the Chairman, Letters from the Public; Records of the National Commission on Law Observance and Enforcement, Record Group 10; National Archives at College Park, College Park, MD.

69. Editorial, *The Cleveland Press*, March 13, 1928; Teapot Dome Files, 226-016, Sub 1; General Records of the Department of Justice, Record Group 60; National Archives at College Park, College Park, MD.

About the National Archives: A Word to Educators

The National Archives and Records Administration (NARA) is responsible for the preservation and use of the permanently valuable records of the federal government. These materials provide evidence of the activities of the government from 1774 to the present in the form of written and printed documents, maps and posters, sound recordings, photographs, films, computer tapes, and other media. These rich archival sources are useful to everyone: federal officials seeking information on past government activities, citizens needing data for use in legal matters, historians, social scientists and public policy planners, environmentalists, historic preservationists, medical researchers, architects and engineers, novelists and playwrights, journalists researching stories, students preparing papers, and persons tracing their ancestry or satisfying their curiosity about particular historical events. These records are useful to you as educators either in preparing your own instructional materials or pursuing your own research.

The National Archives records are organized by the governmental body that created them rather than under a library's subject/author/title categories. There is no Dewey decimal or Library of Congress designation; each departmental bureau or collection of agency's records is assigned a record group number. In lieu of a card catalog, inventories and other finding aids assist the researcher in locating material in records not originally created for research purposes, often consisting of thousands of cubic feet of documentation.

The National Archives is a public institution whose records and research facilities nationwide are open to anyone 14 years of age and over. These facilities are found in the Washington, DC, metropolitan area, in the 11 Presidential libraries, the Nixon Presidential Materials Project, and in 16 regional archives across the nation. Whether you are pursuing broad historical questions or are interested in the history of your family, admittance to the research room at each location requires only that you fill out a simple form stating your name, address, and research interest. A staff member then issues an identification card, which is good for two years.

If you come to do research, you will be offered an initial interview with a reference archivist. You will also be able to talk with archivists who have custody of the records. If you have a clear definition of your questions and have prepared in advance by reading as many of the secondary sources as possible, you will find that these interviews can be very helpful in guiding you to the research material you need.

The best printed source of information about the overall holdings of the National Archives is the *Guide to the National Archives of the United States* (issued in 1974, reprinted in 1988), which is available in university libraries and many public libraries and online at **www.nara.gov**. The *Guide* describes in very general terms the records in the National Archives, gives the background and history of each agency represented by those records, and provides useful information about access to the records. To accommodate users outside of Washington, DC, the regional archives hold microfilm copies of much that is found in Washington. In addition, the regional archives contain records created by field offices of the federal government, including district and federal appellate court records, records of the Bureau of Indian Affairs, National Park Service, Bureau of Land Management, Forest Service, Bureau of the Census, and others. These records are particularly useful for local and regional history studies and in linking local with national historical events.

For more information about the National Archives and its educational and cultural programs, visit NARA's Web site at **www.nara.gov**.

Presidential Libraries

Herbert Hoover Library
210 Parkside Drive
West Branch, IA 52358-0488
319-643-5301

Franklin D. Roosevelt Library
511 Albany Post Road
Hyde Park, NY 12538-1999
914-229-8114

Harry S. Truman Library
500 West U.S. Highway 24
Independence, MO 64050-1798
816-833-1400

Dwight D. Eisenhower Library
200 Southeast Fourth Street
Abilene, KS 67410-2900
785-263-4751

John Fitzgerald Kennedy Library
Columbia Point
Boston, MA 02125-3398
617-929-4500

Lyndon Baines Johnson Library
2313 Red River Street
Austin, TX 78705-5702
512-916-5137

Gerald R. Ford Library
1000 Beal Avenue
Ann Arbor, MI 48109-2114
734-741-2218

Jimmy Carter Library
441 Freedom Parkway
Atlanta, GA 30307-1498
404-331-3942

Ronald Reagan Library
40 Presidential Drive
Simi Valley, CA 93065-0600
805-522-8444/800-410-8354

George Bush Library
1000 George Bush Drive
P.O. Box 10410
College Station, TX 77842-0410
409-260-9552

Clinton Presidential Materials Project
1000 LaHarpe Boulevard
Little Rock, AR 72201
501-254-6866

National Archives Regional Archives

NARA-Northeast Region
380 Trapelo Road
Waltham, MA 02452-6399
781-647-8104

NARA-Northeast Region
10 Conte Drive
Pittsfield, MA 01201-8230
413-445-6885

NARA-Northeast Region
201 Varick Street, 12th Floor
New York, NY 10014-4811
212-337-1300

NARA-Mid Atlantic Region
900 Market Street
Philadelphia, PA 19107-4292
215-597-3000

NARA-Mid Atlantic Region
14700 Townsend Road
Philadelphia, PA 19154-1096
215-671-9027

NARA-Southeast Region
1557 St. Joseph Avenue
East Point, GA 30344-2593
404-763-7474

NARA-Great Lakes Region
7358 South Pulaski Road
Chicago, IL 60629-5898
773-581-7816

NARA-Great Lakes Region
3150 Springboro Road
Dayton, OH 45439-1883
937-225-2852

NARA-Central Plains Region
2312 East Bannister Road
Kansas City, MO 64131-3011
816-926-6272

NARA-Central Plains Region
200 Space Center Drive
Lee's Summit, MO 64064-1182
816-478-7079

NARA-Southwest Region
501 West Felix Street
P.O. Box 6216
Fort Worth, TX 76115-0216
817-334-5525

NARA-Rocky Mountain Region
Denver Federal Center, Building 48
P.O. Box 25307
Denver, CO 80225-0307
303-236-0804

NARA-Pacific Region
24000 Avila Road
P.O. Box 6719
Laguna Niguel, CA 92607-6719
949-360-2641

NARA-Pacific Region
1000 Commodore Drive
San Bruno, CA 94066-2350
650-876-9009

NARA-Pacific Alaska Region
6125 Sand Point Way, NE
Seattle, WA 98115-7999
206-526-6507

NARA-Pacific Alaska Region
654 West Third Avenue
Anchorage, AK 99501-2145
907-271-2443

Reproductions of Documents

Reproductions of the oversized print documents included in these units are available in their original size by special order from Graphic Visions.

25 Miles *to the* Gallon

Startling good news to tens of thousands—the first announcements of the new good Maxwell's amazing results. Never since the Chrysler took the country by storm has the automobile industry known such whole-hearted response—such a dramatic and decisive triumph.

Not content with designing into this car power and pick-up equaled only in the higher priced fields, Chrysler engineering genius and fine manufacturing facilities enable the new good Maxwell owner to enjoy these performance advantages with unparalleled economy.

In almost sensationally low cost of operation and maintenance—as in speed and acceleration—this great car has written a wholly new page in motor car achievement, and in the accomplishment of the great organization which builds the Maxwell.

58 Miles *per* Hour

5 to 25 Miles *in 8 Seconds*

MAXWELL

Balloon tires, natural wood wheels, stop-light, transmission lock, Duco finish *standard* on all Maxwell models. Shrouded visor integral with roof; heater, standard on all closed models.

Touring Car	- - - $895	Standard Four-Door Sedan $1095
Club Coupe -	- - - - 995	Special Four-Door Sedan - 1245

All prices f. o. b. Detroit, tax extra

There are Maxwell dealers and superior Maxwell service everywhere. All dealers are in position to extend the convenience of time-payments. Ask about Maxwell's attractive plan.

The New Good MAXWELL

Document 1. Maxwell Car Ad, *The Literary Digest*, April 11, 1925. [National Archives]

Document 2. Cartoon, Chicago *Daily Tribune*, August 23, 1924.

Girl, Boy, Bottle And Auto Most Dangerous Quartet, Says Educator

School Head Fears Destruction Of Society in Code Of Modern Youth

CHICAGO, April 18. (AP)—Edward J. Tobin, superintendent of Cook county schools and in that capacity supervisor over the schooling of 100,000 children, believes that "a young couple a bottle of moonshine and an automobile are the most dangerous quartet that can be concocted for the destruction of human society."

Tobin is one of six men, prominent in education in Cook county, who are acting as jurors in the coroner's investigation of George Lux's death early Sunday after a round of roadhouses with several other young men and girls.

His views were epitomized in six paragraphs, as follows:

About 70 percent of the young men of 18 to 25 years of age accept as the regular standard recreation a party, an auto ride, dancing and a bottle of gin or moonshine.

Bottle Dictates Habits

About 50 to 60 percent of the girls above 17 years of age accept this code.

In pre-volstead days the bottle never aspired to dictate the social habits of our young people. It does today.

A young couple, a bottle of moonshine and a automobile are the most dangerous quartet that can be concocted for the destruction of human society.

Families and homes originate from early asociation of young people of both sexes. A home or a family tied with a bottle of bootleg has a foundation in quicksand.

The bottle is a by product of prohibition, either the bottle as one of the trio has got to go or its ancestor, prohibition, must go.

The school superintendent gave it as his opinion that the liquor and delinquency problem among American youth rested first with parents, then with schools and finally with the law.

Prof. S. N. Stevens of the Department of Psychology at Northwestern, another member of the jury, expressed the opinion that no one factor is responsible for present conditions in the moral and social life of youth.

He said social instability inherited from the war was one factor; changing economic conditions and larger social freedom for women others. He touched upon the failure of parents to do their full duty, and he said that "the churches have been more interested in maintaining themselvs as institutions than in creating a larger opportunity for the development of a satisfying life on the part of their people."

As a remedy he sugested the need of recreation in the home and "a new devlopment of family interests and enthusiasms."

He said also that "youth itself must come to realize that it is the carrier of the social traditions, that in a very large measure society and civilization in the future depend upon its intellectual and moral integrity."

REPORT OF METROPOLITAN POLICE DEPARTMENT

Vincennes, Indiana, January 1, 1923.

To the Honorable Board of Police Commissioners of the City of Vincennes, Indiana.

We have the honor to submit to you for your consideration and approval the annual report of the Metropolitan Police Department of the City of Vincennes, Indiana, for the year ending December 31, 1922.

Adultry	16
Assault and Battery	70
All other Misdemeanors	16
Bastardy	3
Carrying concealed weapons	8
Drawing deadly weapons	5
Delinquency	2
Deserter	1
Deserting child and wife	2
Forgery	10
Fornication	6
Fugitive	6
Gambling	59
Grand Larceny	11
Intoxication	285
Insanity	5
Incest	1
Non support	12
No tail light	9
Provoke	8
Petit Larceny	36
Prostitution and Associating	27
Riot	4
Rape	3
Suspicion	3
Surety of Peace	1
Speeding	87
Violation of Liquor Law	111
Vagrancy	4
Vehicle taking	3
Total number of arrests	**814**

Document 4. Report of metropolitan police department, *17th Annual Reports of Departments*, 1922, Vincennes, IN. [National Archives]

Document 5. Photograph from Hood River County, OR, July 20, 1925. [National Archives]

Phila: Pa.

7/22/29

Mr Wickersham;
Dear Sir,

    Please hear the plea of a heartbroken
mother and send some reliable person to investigate the
 condition of an Italian joint,where children are sold rum
for ten cents a drink. My boy with several companions Went
swimming and after the swim they suggested he go with them
to get something to warm them up consquently my thirteen
year old boy was brought home to me in a drunken stupor.

    Willingly would I send you his name but I dread the
publicity his father is dead I am alone trying to rear him
an honorable American but how canI when this foreigner I
doubt if he has ever been naturlized is allowed to ruin my
boy.

    The City wont close him up he has been arrested
several times,he keeps right on doing business,he has been
in this vicinity for the last six years and in this present
location the last three.

    This Italian is known by the name of Nick he had a
shack at 63 and Lindberg Boulevard a man bought the ground
put up a Sun Gasoline Station and knowing that he sold rum
built him a resturant right in the station that is where
my boy bought his, then they moved the old shack across
the road and that is where it is hid in and around the
old shack.

    Send one of your men to 63 &Lindberg Boulevard on
the Back Road stay around that Sun Station watch the Res_
turant an the shack across the road, noon hour is a good
time that is when I went down to remonstrate with him
never in my life did I meet with such insults he was
surrounded with bums and ordered me out under threat that
he would have one of them throw me out, I dont know why I
didnt kill him. I am desperate no one can touch him so I
come to you last with my plea please help save these boys
from that poisoned rum.

    My boy is a good boy a pupil of the Tilden Junior
High and carried off the highest honors in his class
last term.

Truly Yours.

A Mother

Document 6. Letter to Mr. [George W.] Wickersham, July 22, 1929. [National Archives]

WESTERN UNION
TELEGRAM

Form 1204

NEWCOMB CARLTON, PRESIDENT   GEORGE W. E. ATKINS, FIRST VICE-PRESIDENT

RECEIVED AT

1OW PV 211 NL 14 EXTRA

SENATE CORRIDOR PHONE BRANCH &?

CLEVELAND OHIO JUNE 26 1919

THOMAS R MARSHALL

VICE PRESIDENT OF THE UNITEDSTATES WASHINGTON DC

THE NATIONAL ASSOCIATION FOR THE ADVANCEMENT OF COLORED PEOPLE IN SESSION

IN CLEVELAND OHIO REPRESENTING TEN MILLION NEGROES OF THE UNITEDSTATES

DEMANDS THE DISPATCH OF FEDERAL TROOPS TO THE STATE OF MISSISSIPPI FOR

THE PROTECTION OF UNITEDSTATES CITIZENS FROM ANARCHY AND MOB VIOLENCE

THE GOVERNOR OF THE STATE HAVING ADMITTED TODAY JUNE 26TH THAT HE IS

POWERLESS TO AFFORD SUCH PROTECTION COMMENTING UPON THE HANGING AND

BURNING WITHOUT ANY PROCESS OF LAW OF JOHN HARTFIELD AT ELLISVILLE MISS

GOVERNOR THEODORE G BILBO IS QUOTED IN THE PRESS AS HAVING SAID "THE

STATE HAS NO TROOPS AND IF THE CIVIL AUTHORITIES AT ELLISVILLE ARE

Form 1204

WESTERN UNION
TELEGRAM

NEWCOMB CARLTON, PRESIDENT   GEORGE W. E. ATKINS, FIRST VICE-PRESIDENT

RECEIVED AT

1OW PV 211 NL 14 EXTRA   SHEET TWO.

SENATE CORRIDOR PHONE BRANCH 47

HELPLESS THE STATE IS EQUALLY SO" AS THIS IS THE SIXTH MOB MURDER IN

MISSISSIPPI SINCE JANUARY FOR WHICH THE STATE OF MISSISSIPPI HAS PROVIDED

NO PUNISHMENT OR PREVENTIVE AND AS UNDER SIMILAR CIRCUMSTANCE THE GOVERNO!

OF NORTHCAROLINA LAST NOVEMBER PREVENTED A LYNCHING THROUGH THE

DISPATCH OF UNITEDSTATES TROOPS TO WINSTON-SALEM THE NATIONAL ASSN

FOR THE ADVANCEMENT OF COLORED PEOPLE DEMANDS THE MAINTENANCE OF

FEDERAL TROOPS IN MISSISSIPPI UNTIL SUCH TIME AS THE STATE OF MISSISS-

IPPI MAY BE ABLE TO AFFORD THE PROTECTION GUARANTEED UNITEDSTATES CITI-

ZENS UNDER THE CONSTITUTION

JOHN R SHILLADY,   SECY THE NATL ASSN FOR THE

ADVANCEMENT OF COLORED

PEOPLE HOTEL HOLLENDED
CLEVELAND OHIO

945AM

Document 7. Telegram from John R. Shillady, Secretary, NAACP,
to Thomas R. Marshall, June 26, 1919. [National Archives]

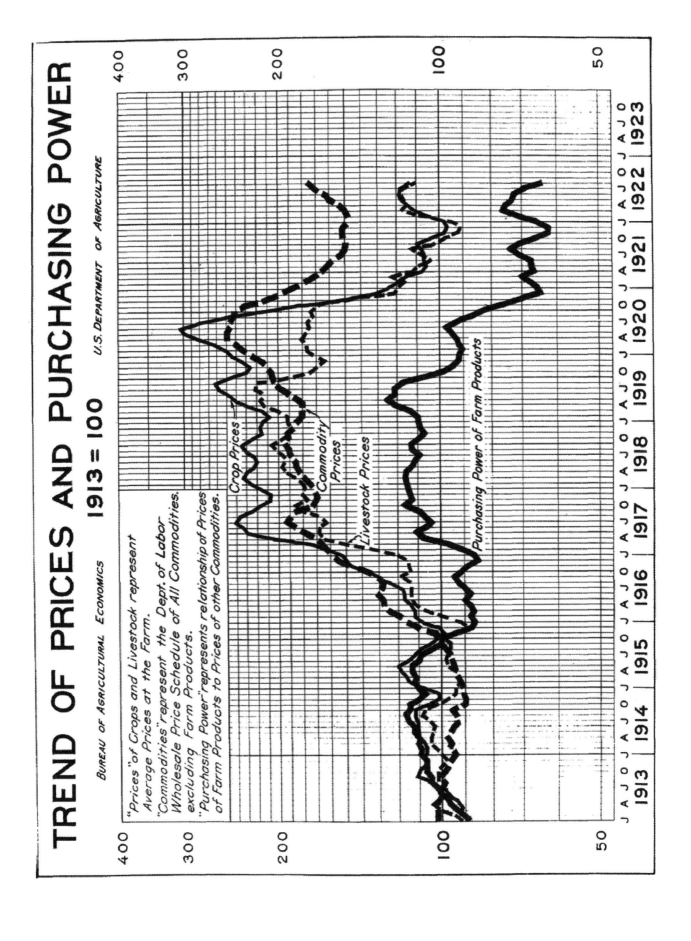

Document 8. Graph of trend of prices and purchasing power, n.d. [National Archives]

Local Union No. 3519,

United Mine Workers of America, District 2.

Bennington, Pa.

 R/F/D/No.1/Gallitzin, Pa Dec. 9th. -20. 191

The Hon. Philander C. Knox,   United States Senate,
Washington, D. C.

WHEREAS, The Signing of the Peace Treaty finds in America civil
and military prisons, or under bail pending trial or appeal, large
numbers of men and women whose offense is of a political nature; and
WHEREAS, The sole justification for such prosecution and impri-
son ment, that of war-time necessity, no longer exists;

WHEREAS, In all democratic countries of Europe which have been
associated with us in the prosecution of the war, full amnesty has
been granted; be it

RESOLVED, that it is the sense of the Membership Of Local
Union No. 3519 United Mine Workers Of America, located at Bennington,
Pa. that the further prosecution and imprisonment in the United
States of Political Offenders is contrary to the democratic idealism
and traditions of freedom to which our country is committed; and be
it further

RESOLVED, that we accordingly urge upon the President of the
United States, upon the Attorney General of the United States, the
Secretary of War, and the American Federation of Labor to make all
efforts possible to secure the granting of amnesty to all persons
whose political beliefs, formed the basis of prosecution, trial and
imprisonment, and be it further

RESOLVED, that we accordingly urge upon the United States
Senators and Representatives to support Joint Resolution for amnesty
and to repeal the Espionage Law.

R. A. Craford Pres.

S. A. Nelson Sec.-Treas.

gl. situation

A. O. Fisher & Co.

MANUFACTURERS OF

CIGAR BOXES

818 & 820 NORTH FRANKLIN ST. Chicago Ill. Aug. 15 1923

Mr. Wallace,
  Secretary of Agriculture,
  Washington, D. C.

Dear Sir:

   I noticed an article in this morning's Chicago newspapers
in which the President is quoted as feeling the greatest sympathy
for the farmer. In my estimation they deserve no sympathy any more
than I do in my business. When I was out west in 1915 I noticed
signs in every railroad station and hotel throughout Montana in
which the British government offered to pay $1.50 per bushel for
wheat, which at that time was a splendid price. The farmers prospered
from that time on until about a year ago; during a certain period
they received between $2.50 and $3.50 per bushel. They should not
expect such prices to continue indefinitely. Had the farmer laid
aside and saved his money when he was getting high prices for his
grain he would be in a position to-day to stand a loss, if necessary.
My business has been poor during the past year, but I am asking for
no financial assistance, nor do I expect it, and neither should the
farmer.

            Yours very truly,

            Albert O. Fisher

Document 10. Letter to Mr. [Henry A.] Wallace from
Albert O. Fisher, August 15, 1923. [National Archives]

FOUNDED 1882

THE WALL STREET JOURNAL.

MORNING AND EVENING EDITION
Published twice daily, except Sundays, by

DOW, JONES & CO.

C. W. BARRON, President.
Hugh Bancroft, Secretary.   Joseph Cashman, Treasurer.
44 Broad Street, New York.
Telephone: Broad One.

Subscriptions: $18 yearly; $1.50 monthly; or seven cents daily, for either edition, postage paid in the United States, Canada, Mexico, Puerto Rico, Guam, Philippine Islands, Hawaiian Islands and Cuba. Foreign postage $4 a year additional.

Subscriptions also received at Washington Bureau, 1422 F Street, N. W.; Chicago Bureau, Room 854, 208 So. La Salle Street.

Addresses changed on request; always give old address.

Advertisements: Rates will be furnished by us or any responsible advertising agency.

Entered as second-class matter August 4, 1913, at the post office at New York, N. Y., under the Act of March 3, 1879

This Paper Has a Larger Circulation Than Any other American Financial Publication.
September 27, 1921.

The truth in its proper use.

A LEGACY FROM MEXICO

Twenty-nine years ago a visitor from Mexico appeared in Brownsville, Texas. It was a harmless-looking fly, not at all unlike a housefly, but grayer. The housekeeper, in swatting the insect, might have remarked that it looked pale and anaemic. It was really more formidable than a Mexican army with German officers. It was the boll weevil. The fly lays its eggs in the blossom of the cotton plant. These develop into a maggot perhaps three-eighths of an inch long. The weevil has spread steadily north until it has invaded our whole cotton belt. Flushed with triumph the fly has grown more adroit and destructive, for it now attacks the cotton boll itself as well as the blossom.

Thanks to the higher price of cotton and the carry-over from last year the South is now in a better financial condition. With twenty-cent cotton the clamor for the complete suppression of the cotton exchanges has died down, for the cotton growers are not quarrelling with a good market. A big cotton crop ultimately helps everybody, even with a low price. A short crop helps those who have the cotton. The farmer's notes for this year are being paid off and part of last year's are being redeemed. The ginners and the cotton factors are more cheerful. But what of the future?

On plantations in Georgia, South Carolina, and parts of the cotton belt remote from the original area of the boll weevil, the destruction has been almost total. In Georgia a planter of ability and resources reports perhaps five bales from two hundred acres. In that district only a fair crop would be a hundred bales. Districts which escaped the boll weevil saw the cotton destroyed by the drought. Some of these parched bolls are scarcely an inch across, with the husk burned like cured tobacco and the lint not worth ginning. Perhaps a little of the fiber may be secured by old-fashioned threshing. This is the condition among farmers and planters who have learned from the Department of Agriculture, and can turn to diversified crops. But what of the negroes and the small farmers who know nothing but cotton? This is the danger to the South, for these people have not the money to buy winter clothes or to insure the planting for next year's crop.

The danger to the South is a panic among these small farmers, and it is a danger to the whole country. The banks, the factors, the ginners and the larger growers can take care of themselves. But this class, happy-go-lucky, shiftless and hand-to-mouth, is almost in danger of extinction. Such as they are the country cannot afford to lose them. They are a national difficulty, a problem much more serious than the sturdy vagabonds in unemployed parades. Suppose Congress turns its attention to them for a little while? At least they have votes, if they are not concerned in, or likely to be benefited by, projects to wreck the cotton exchanges.

COOPERATIVE EXTENSION WORK
IN
AGRICULTURE AND HOME ECONOMICS
STATE OF TEXAS

RICULTURAL AND MECHANICAL COLLEGE

TEXAS AND UNITED STATES DEPARTMENT

OF AGRICULTURE COOPERATING

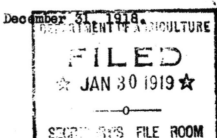

College Station, Texas,

December 31, 1918.

Mr. Bradford Knapp,

      Washington, D. C.

Dear Mr. Knapp:

      During the last few weeks I have heard a number of expressions
that convinced me that the returned negro soldier will likely prove a
very great problem in many communities in the south. This is a question,
that so far as I am aware, has not been given the consideration that
its importance demands, and unless some active steps are taken at once
to bring our people to a better understanding and more sympathetic appreciation of the situation of the returned negro soldier, I fear that
in many communities in the South we will witness some of the disgrace-
ful spectacles that have been so common in our section of the country
since the civil war.

      It occurs to me that the Extension Division of the various
Colleges might be able to render the War Department some service in
assisting in bringing this matter to the attention of the citizens,
both white and black. As an illustration of such difficulties; just
a few days ago in a nearby county, two negro boys returned from one
of the camps and were thoroughly beaten by a bunch of white boys
because they thought the negro boys were not quite as humble as they
should have been, and the white boys had gotten the impression that
it was their specific duty to keep the negro in his place. I know
that it will not be possible to prevent some difficulties along this
line and I fear there will be much difficulty unless there is some
kind of educational campaign outlined that will bring to the attention
of our citizens more forcibly than has been done, the positive responsibility of our white people in seeing to it that the negro gets a
square deal. I do not mean to convey the impression that the negro
should not be made to keep in a negro's place, but I wish to say that
I am of the positive opinion that we owe a very direct responsibility
to the negro, and those of us who are in a position to lend our influence towards the prevention of difficulties, should do so. It
occurs to me that if arrangements could be made through the War Department for the right kind of negroes to meet negro soldiers at points
of demobilization and talk with them both in public and private, much
might be accomplished that way. As an illustration of what I mean,
I refer to the riots of the negro soldiers at Houston some 18 months

Mr. Knapp - - -#2

ago and to the work of E. L. Blackshear in assisting to control
that very delicate and difficult situation. Immediately upon
receiving information as to what had occurred, Blackshear got
permission to address negro soldiers in the camps, also the
negro population near the camps, and I have positive information
that his efforts were of material assistance in preventing further
difficulties. If some plan could be worked out by which men like
Blackshear and others of his race could present their views to
returning negro soldiers, it would surely prevent some serious
difficulties that are likely to occur unless some such step is
taken.

Yours very truly,

T. O. Walton

Acting Director.

TOW:M.

"BROOKLYN STANDARD UNION"

ON: WEDNESDAY, MARCH 23, 1921.

SAYS THE FOREIGNER IS NOT APPRECIATED

Immigration Not a Menace to Nation, Says Commissioner Wallis.

TALKS AT UNIVERSITY CLUB.

Thinks U. S. Agents Should Select Immigrants Abroad.

Commissioner of Immigration Frederick A. Wallis told the members and guests of the University Club, Lafayette avenue, last night, that the solution of the immigration problem lay, not in such tests as the literary test, which he said was not worth a snap, but in the selection of the immigrant on the other side by American inspectors and the scientific distribution and sensible amalgamation of the new citizen on this side of the water.

"I have never thought of immigration as a national menace," the Commissioner said. "I believe the problem can best be met by scientific selection of the immigrant on the other side and the safe and sensible distribution here.

"We don't appreciate the foreigner —that's the trouble with us. We look upon him as a foreigner. Well, he is; we all are, no matter how far back we trace our blood, unless you happen to be an Indian.

"One thing the war has brought to us on Ellis Island is that we don't see much difference between the immigrant of to-day and the early immigrants whom we call Pilgrims. You look upon the incoming foreigner as a common mechanic, as a laborer, an artisan. Yet he has risen to the positions of preacher, doctor, officer, and even member of the Cabinet. The immigrant, if well selected, will bring to the country strong arms, a keen eye, balanced brain and an almost superhuman ability to work."

What the Immigrant Does.

The immigrant, according to the Commissioner, contributes 85 per cent. of all labor in the meat-packing industries; nine-tenths in the cotton mills, nine-twentieths in the clothing, one-half in the shoes, one-half in the collars, four-fifths in the leather, one-half in the gloves, nine-twentieths in the refining of sugar and one-half in the tobacco and cigarette industries. "And yet they call the immigrant the 'great American problem!' "

"I believe in a certain kind of immigration. The immigrant is indispensable to our industries. However, we do not care for the foreigner who thinks his first task here is to get up on a soapbox or up in a public school and, preach the overthrow of the Government."

Speaking on the Americanization of the newcomer to this country, he thought Americanization could no longer be "shoved and crammed down the throats of the foreigner any more than a preacher can shove religion down anyone's throat.

The Way to Americanization.

"The way to Americanization is through patience, not pressure," he warned. "It must come by environment, by better home and living conditions. In this respect the first impression is an important one. Conditions at Ellis Island should be made as comfortable and pleasing as possible. For that reason we are trying to humanize the island; trying to put more sunlight there.

Commissioner Wallis surprised his audience when he informed them that there is a well-established stowaway system in operation from Greek and other Mediterranean ports to Liverpool, thence to America.

"I believe the medical examinations of to-day are farces," Commissioner Wallis continued. "The examination is superficial. Many pass through with governmental permission who are diseased inwardly with no ap-

3/26 To Com'r Genl Immigration   KHc

Document 13. "Says the Foreigner is not Appreciated," Brooklyn *Standard Union*, March 23, 1921. [National Archives]

GOLF COURSES LAID OUT AND CONSTRUCTED

GRADING	MACADAM TENNIS COURTS	LAKE CONSTRUCTION	LANDSCAPE WORK
	MACADAM, CONCRETE AND ASPHALT ROAD CONSTRUCTION		
CRUSHED AND BUILDING STONE		MASONRY AND CONCRETE WORK	HAULING
STEAM ROLLERS	PORTABLE STEAM SHOVELS	PORTABLE CRUSHER	MOTOR TRUCKS

R. H. JOHNSON COMPANY
CONTRACTORS

F. A. CANIZARES, Pres.-Treas.
O. L. DUNNE, Vice President
A. W. CANIZARES, Secretary
MICHAEL CIVITELLO, Manager

BRANCH OFFICE
Wilmington, Del.

Wayne, Penna., September 20th., 1922.

The Honorable Secretary of Labor,

    Washington, D. C.

Sir,

    Enclosed herewith please find copy of letter sent our representative, the Honorable Thomas S. Butler.

    This section around Philadelphia is over 50% short of the necessary common labor to do the normal amount of building now in progress, and will be very much more shortened as the Sesqui-Centennial works proceed.

    It is absolutely vital to those interested in housing, the building trades and all contractors, that something be immediately done to let in European labor of the proper type to do these works.

    The derelicts which are loafing around your employment agencies in Philadelphia, and elsewhere, will not do excavation work, and the sooner the labor bureau realizes that Americans will not do work of this character, and admit a sufficient quantity of labor to do it, the sooner prices will be stabilized and assume a proper level, and in addition, a large proportion of strikes would be eliminated if there were some COMPETITION FOR THE JOB.

    Please get some action in this matter as it is imperative, and oblige,

Yours very respectfully,
R. H. JOHNSON COMPANY.

President.

CONTRACTS AND AGREEMENTS MADE CONTINGENT UPON GOVERNMENT ORDERS, FIRES, STRIKES, ACCIDENTS, UNCERTAIN TRANSPORTATION AND OTHER CAUSES BEYOND OUR CONTROL. PRICES ARE BASED UPON COST OF LABOR AT DATE OF QUOTATION, AND ARE SUBJECT TO CHANGE. ROCK OF ALL KINDS AND QUICKSAND WORK EXTRA.

Document 14. Letter to the Hon. Secretary of Labor, Washington, DC, from F. A. Canizares, September 20, 1922. [National Archives]

LOGGIA BEATRICE CENCI NO. 1207

ELIZABETH, N. J., ———————— February 9th 192⁴

United State Senate,
Washington, D.C.

Gentlemen:-

  The Lodge Beatrice Cenci, No. 1207, of the Order of Sons of Italy in America, whose members are wives and daughters of citizens, do hereby respectfully submit for your kind consideration the following statement, as a protest to the passage of the law, proposed by Congressman Johnson, restricting the Italian Immigration to the United States.

 ** The greatness of this Country is principally due to Immigration.

 ** The Italian immigrants are able-bodied, honest and hard workmen and never refused to work in difficult and dangerous undertaking, such as mines, railways, bridges, subways, buildings and so on, even at cost of their lives.

 ** During the World War, Italians of any age and trade fought shoulder by shoulder with Americans for justice and liberty.

 ** This proposed act, if approved and passed, will close the doors of this country to a friend people and open them to nations, who fought against our fathers, husbands and sons.

 ** We are not looking for freetrade, but we want to see the lands and farms of this big country developed and cultivated. We must build hour homes and buy necessities of life at a reasonable cost.

LOGGIA BEATRICE CENCI NO. 1207

ELIZABETH, N. J._____192

- 2 -

We are not writing this letter for selfishness, but because, as
wives and daughters of American citizens, we wish to eliminate
graft, monopolies and crimes and bring better conditions at home.

Very respectfully yours

Caterina Tripodi

Venerabile

Maria L. Guidi

Secy of Corr.

Alliance, Ohio, May #5,1924.

President Calvin Coolidge,
Washington, D.C.

Honored Sir,-

    We, the Women of the Ku Klux Klan of
Alliance, Ohio, do so heartily approve the Johnson
Immigration Bill so overwhalmingly passed by House
and Senate, and we earnestly request that you, the
President of this United States, give your support
and affix your signature to this bill.

    We shall ever be devoted to the sublime
principals of a pure Americanism, and valiant in the
defense of its' ideals and institutions.

    It is our earnest desire to promote real
patriotism toward our civil government, honorable
peace among men and nations, and protection for and
happiness in the homes of our people.

                        Sincerely,
                        Alliance Klan # 1,
                        Women of the Ku Klux Klan.

Document 16. Letter to President Calvin Coolidge from
Alliance Klan #1, May 15, 1924. [National Archives]

Document 17. Photograph, "Ellis Island, NY," 1923. [National Archives]

The
Colored American Council
(INCORPORATED)

1215 SEVENTEENTH STREET, N. W.

WASHINGTON D.C.

17)20   February 14,1920.

Hon. Woodrow Wilson,
   President of the United States,
      Executive Mansion,
         Washington, D.C..

Dear Sir:
      In connection with the threatened railroad
strike, I am prompted to invite the attention of the
President to the possibilities of the elimination of
the costly separate car passenger service maintained
by Federal taxation in the Southern interstate traffic
district.

      This service is supported by governmental guar-
antee at an annual cost of twenty five million dollars
($25,000,000) which estimate does not include four states
using the service out credited to the western district.

      It serves no useful,American purpose but forms
according to current opinion a fertile field for propaganda aimed at national disintegration. Its elimination
would free for wage increases to railway workers,$25,000,
000.

      On its face its elimination constitutes a pro-
posal which is at once fair to the roads, the railworkers
and the American people. It is an economy which requires
no outlay of capital to effect and I trust that your
Excellency will give its possibilities due consideration.

                              George A. Murray.

                              General Counsel.

Document 18. Letter to the Hon. Woodrow Wilson from
George A. Murray, February 14, 1920. [National Archives]

JOHN T. ADAMS
CHAIRMAN

FRED W. UPHAM
TREASURER

C. B. HEIER.
SECRETARY

REPUBLICAN NATIONAL COMMITTEE

H. L. REMMEL
MEMBER OF ARKANSAS

LITTLE ROCK, ARKANSAS

October 3, 1923.

Hon. Henry C. Wallace,
Secretary of Agriculture,
Washington, D. C.

My dear Mr. Wallace:

On Saturday last I had a conference with President Coolidge and, among other things, I took up with him the question of emigration of the colored man from the south to the north.

This has become a very acute question in the south, as many thousands of colored men and their families have gone north, in many instances leaving their cotton fields with the crop half cultivated, selling what few goods they can and going north, leaving the planters without labor to cultivate their fields. It has been stated through the press that as many as 150,000 colored people have gone to the north during 1923, some reports making it even more. This is of vital importance to our planters and farmers, as the colored man and his family constitute practically the agricultural labor in the alluvial bottom lands of all of our southern states. The uplands or mountain regions are occupied by white people.

I suggested to the President that he appoint a commission of say five colored men of recognized experience and ability and men of good intelligence to constitute a commission and to make their headquarters at Tuskegee, Alabama, where the Booker Washington school has been sending out young colored men, trained in scientific agriculture and mechanics and women in domestic science; then these commissions visit southern states at different times, calling conferences and conventions and discussing with the colored people the importance of diversified farming and to tell them that the south is the natural home of the colored man and his family.

                                                                    southern
These colored commissioners must be men of recognized worth and merit in the com-munities from which they hailed and be practical agriculturalists. The President seemed favorably impressed with my suggestions. I told him that I had previously discussed this same matter with President Harding and he, also was favorably impressed with the idea and thought he would appoint such a commission.

President Coolidge requested me to call on you and discuss the situation as I had with him. I told him that I would have to leave that evening and would not have time to discuss the merits of my recommendation, but would write you, and that is what I am doing now. Since my return home I have had a number of white men, as well as colored men, write me and also phone me, and some have called at my office, saying that they thought my plan a good one. I would appreciate it very much, my dear Mr. Secretary, if you would consider these suggestions and let me know your views in the matter.

Yours very truly,

H L Remmel

Document 19. Letter to the Hon. Henry C. Wallace from
H. L. Remmel, October 3, 1923. [National Archives]

54940

United States Post Office

Marshall, Texas.

_____ CLASS

July 17, 1919.

Honorable Third Assistant,
Division of Classification,
Washington, D. C.

I beg to submit for your consideration a copy
of the "Chicago Defender," published in Chicago, Ill.,
and entered as second-class mail matter, with the view of
ascertaining if publications of this character are entitled to second-class entry:

I am moved to submit this case because of the
recent happenings at Longview, Texas, county seat of
Gregg County, 24 miles west of Marshall.   From the
enclosed copies of the Dallas News, Shreveport Times and
Marshall Messenger, you will note that quite a race riot
has occurred at that point.

The inception of this trouble was caused by an
article published in this same "Chicago Defender," in
which the character of a reputable white woman was defamed.
This kind of matter will absolutely not go in this section
of the country. And any publication printing these kind
of stories is thereby doing everything possible to stir
up strife and trouble for the negroes.

If you will note the copy enclosed, you will
see that this publication panders to the worst impulses
of the negro race in attempting to cause animosity against
the whites. This course if pursued will eventually cause
trouble wherever the publication comes to the attention
of the reputable citizens of the communities affected.

I have lived in this county all my life, and
I wish to state without any reservation that nowhere in
the world are the negroes treated more fairly or better
than right here in this section; BUT, whenever any
aspersion is cast on white women by inflammatory publications
issued in the interests of the negroes, trouble will
ensue and right rapidly.

The trouble at Longview has caused loss of life,
martial law in that city, and a great deal of unwholesome
notoriety for this section; and all on account of the
publication by the "Chicago Defender " of an article

which is an infamous lie written by some irresponsible negro.

These same papers are being circulated by both mail list and by agent in Marshall, and so acute was the tension here that the Sheriff warned the agent as to sale of these papers, and by order of the agent, received his bundle of papers for this week.

I do not believe any city in the South has done better for the negroes than has Marshall; we have two large negro institutions of learning here, the Bishop College and Wiley University; both institutions of high standing in educational ranks; and the citizenship of this town has always supported these institutions, both morally and financially.

The negroes of this section are as a rule, a contented people with the exception of a few agitators, among whom will be found supporters of such publications as the "Chicago Defender." I mention these facts that you may not believe it is from any spite this matter is taken up.

I do believe however, and the officials of the law here will second this, that publications of the class of the Defender are inflammatory in their character and do more harm for the negroes than any other one thing.

H. C. Blalock,
Postmaster.

H. C. Blalock

Document 20b. Letter to the Hon. Third Assistant, Division of Classification [U.S. Post Office Department], from H. C. Blalock, July 17, 1919. [National Archives]

UNITED STATES RAILROAD ADMINISTRA[...]

DIRECTOR GENERAL OF RAILROADS

SUBJECT: Alleged discrimination in refusing to sell at Northern points prepaid tickets from points in the South.

June 21, 1919.

MEMORANDUM   for Mr. Hines:

A number of complaints have come to this Division from persons who have endeavored to purchase prepaid tickets at various points in the North with a view to sending them to colored relatives in the South for transportation to northern points.

For instance, on June 3, 1919, Rev. M. C. Bailey, pastor of the Antioch Baptist Church of Cleveland, Ohio, applied at the United States Railway ticket office at Cleveland to purchase a prepaid ticket from Madison, Alabama, to Cleveland, Ohio, which ticket he desired to send to his daughter, Mrs. Lottie Beadle for transportation from Madison, Alabama to Cleveland, Ohio. Rev. Bailey and his daughter are colored. The ticket clerk refused to sell such ticket to Rev. Bailey, stating to him that an order had been issued by the Director General against such practice on the ground that it would encourage colored labor to come North. This particular instance has been the subject of letters from Senator Harding and Representative Emerson of Ohio, and appeared as a news item in the New York Times, New York Post and possibly other papers.

As you will note, the ticket agent is alleged to have stated that his refusal to sell the prepaid ticket was due to an order issued by the Director General. Investigation by this Division develops the fact that a ruling to this effect was made prior to the period of Federal control by the Southern Passenger Association, which ruling has been followed during the period of Federal control.

It appears that the Southern railroads decided that they did not want to have colored labor leaving the South to go to the North and for that reason made the rule to which I have referred. It also appears that with this exception prepaid tickets may be purchased at any ticket office in the United States.

I do not know what right the Southern railroads had to decide that they would throw stumbling blocks in the way of colored persons desiring to travel from the South to the North. Whatever reason may have animated them, it seems to me clear that the Railroad Administration cannot consistently sanction the continuance of such a rule.

rule
I recommend that you give instructions to have this/abrogated.

Max Thelen
Director.

MT*er

Document 21. Memorandum for Mr. [Walker D.] Hines from Max Thelen, June 21, 1919. [National Archives]

Are You Getting Your Share of the Country's Prosperity?

OTHERS ARE, WHY NOT YOU?

We have made many people independent by establishing them in their own homes at our beautiful developments. Let us do the same for you.

The Hegemonian can be built from $1,250 up
Payable $12.50 monthly.

Own your own home, pay for it with your rent at New Brunswick Terrace on the Main Line Pennsylvania Railroad, near the large industrial city of New Brunswick, 55 minutes' ride from New York City, the most prosperous city in the world, and also a short ride from Philadelphia.

**HIGH WAGE SCALE
EQUAL RIGHTS AND
OPPORTUNITIES**

You will not be congested or crowded into slums of large cities or towns where race riots and prejudice are bred. Secure some of our desirable building lots, on easy payments.

When the land is paid for you can have your own home built according to your requirements from $1250 up, payable $12.50 monthly.

If you have any regard for your own or your family's future, do not miss this opportunity.

Last Call for Lots at a Special Price

$69
EACH

Prices on all lots positively increased November 1st.

Send for free illustrated booklet showing modern homes built by us and occupied by Colored people.

HEGEMAN HOMES

The N. T. HEGEMAN COMPANY

We are open for several keen and progressive representatives on salary and commission basis.

Main Office, 9 Church Street, New York City

Document 22. Ad, The Chicago *Defender*, September 27, 1919. [National Archives]

3,000 WILL BURN NEGRO

Kaiser Under Stronger Guard Following Escape Of Crown Prince

Frank Simonds
Writes For States

NEW ORLEANS STATES

VOL. 38. NO 172.   22 PAGES   NEW ORLEANS, LA., THURSDAY, JUNE 26, 1919   PRICE 2 CENTS ETYM

From the Jackson, Miss., Daily News, Thursday, June 26, 1919.

27th YEAR

JOHN HARTFIELD WILL BE LYNCHED BY ELLISVILLE MOB AT 5 O'CLOCK THIS AFTERNOON

Governor Bilbo Says He Is Powerless to Prevent It—Thousands of People Are Flocking Into Ellisville to Attend the Event—Sheriff and Authorities Are Powerless to Prevent It.

HATTIESBURG, June 26.—John Hartfield, the negro alleged to have assaulted an Ellisville, young woman, has been taken to Ellisville and is guarded by officers in the office of Dr. Carter in that city. He is wounded in the shoulder but not seriously. The officers have agreed to turn him over to the people of the city at 4 o'clock this afternoon when it is expected he will be burned. The negro is said to have made a partial confession.

GOV. BILBO SAYS HE IS POWERLESS.

When Gov. Bilbo was shown the above dispatch and asked what action, if any, he intended to take to prevent the affair, he said:

'I am powerless to prevent it. 'We have guns for state militia, but no men. It is impossible to send troops to the scene for the obvious reason that we have no troops

"Several days ago, anticipating

for the lynching has now been fixed for five p. m.

A committee of Ellisville citizens has been appointed to make the necessary arrangements for the event, and the mob is pledged to act in conformity with these arrangements.

Rev. L. G. Gates, pastor of the First Baptist church of Laurel, left here at one o'clock for Ellisville to entreat the mob to use discretion.

THOUSANDS GOING

NEGRO JERKY AND SULLEN AS BURNING HOUR NEARS

To Be Taken to Scene of Crime and Stood Before Crowd

ELLISVILLE, Miss., June 26.—(Special.)—As four o'clock approaches John Hartfield, assailant of the Ellisville white girl, is being carefully guarded in the office of Dr. Carter of this city.

The wounded negro has confessed and seems very nervous.

Dissention has broken out among the indignant citizens as to what disposition should be made of the prisoner.

It is said the negro will be taken to the scene of his crime, near the Ellisville railroad tracks, where he attacked Miss Meek, and will be stood up where everybody can see him.

Some of the angry citizens, it is said, want Hartfield lynched, while others want him burned.

ELLISVILLE, Miss., June 26.—(Special)—Walter Crawley and Will Rogers, two farmers, were members of the posse who shot Hartfield in the shoulder, and affected his capture.

Three thousand strangers are in Ellisville today to witness the disposition of John Hartfield, negro assailant of Miss Meek.

Officers are unable to control the crowds.

HATTIESBURG, Miss., June 26.—John Hartfield, negro assailant of an Ellisville young woman, has been brought to Ellisville from Collins and is guarded by officers in the office of Dr. Carter in that city.

He is wounded in the shoulder. The officers have agreed to turn him over to the people at 4 o'clock this afternoon when it is expected he will be burned.

Document 23. Flyer from the NAACP, n.d. [National Archives]

O. B. Dry Goods Store

MRS. H. LIPSETT
PROPRIETOR

5034 NEWPORT AVENUE
OCEAN BEACH, CALIF.

April 19, 1929

202600-

Department of Justice
Washington, D. C.

Gentlemen:

Do you encourage Bolshevism in this country?
Do you tolerate Bolshevism in the United
States?

If you do then I am awfully sorry to waste
my time in writing and your time in reading
these few lines.

But if you do not (and I am sure that you
do not) then the address which I am enclosing will stand a little investigation and
a great deal of your attention, I presume.

This man has been a stark raving socialist,
social democrat, and at the present time he
is a bolshevik.

He is a born Russian, a Canadian subject,
and for the last seven years he has been
living in Los Angeles.

I do not believe that at the present time
he is taking an active part in any
bolshevik movement, but he has recently
made a will leaving his property to the
Communist party.

Any questions that you care to ask me I
will be glad to answer.

Respectfully yours,

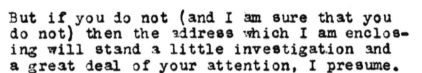

Document 24. Letter to the Department of Justice from Mrs. H. Lipsett, April 19, 1929. [National Archives]

TELEPHONE FRANKLIN 1298

THE BLAKE MANUFACTURING CO.

SOLE MANUFACTURERS OF

VAN GLECKLAND SEMI-PORTABLE ACETYLENE GENERATORS

SPECIAL EQUIPMENTS

LIGHT PORTABLE WELDING GENERATORS
SHOP WELDING--CUTTING GENERATORS
GENERATORS FOR RADIATOR WELDING
GENERATORS FOR LEAD BURNING

AN ABSOLUTELY SAFE ACETYLENE GENERATOR FOR ALL PURPOSES

Welding, Cutting, Lead Burning and Lighting

ADDRESS REPLIES TO
19 South Wells Street, Chicago

SPECIAL EQUIPMENTS

MANTLE BURNING LIGHTING SYSTEMS
PORTABLE CAMP OUTFITS
CONSTRUCTION FLOOD LAMPS
OXYGEN DECARBONIZERS

CHICAGO, Sept. 19, 1919

Walker D. Hines, Director General of Railroads,

United States Railroad Administration,

Washington, D. C.

Dear Sir:

    The writer just returned from Elmira, N. Y. on Michigan Central Train No. 17 and was very much surprised to find that it is now becoming necessary to associate with negro passengers on a so called high grade, excess fare train.

    I am sure you can appreciate the unpleasantness of being compelled to share dressing rooms with the negros.

Yours very truly,

M. W. Briggs

LISTED BY UNDERWRITERS' LABORATORIES—INSPECTED MECHANICAL APPLIANCES

Document 25. Letter to Walker D. Hines from M. W. Briggs, September 19, 1919. [National Archives]

Armstrong Technical High School
Washington, D. C.
June 18, 1922.

Hon. Warren G. Harding,
President of the United States,
The White House,
Washington, D. C.

Dear Sir:

I am taking the liberty of intruding this letter upon you, because I feel that the issues involved are as important as any questions that have ever been pressed upon you. It is to urge your support of the Dyer Bill.

Mr. President, lynching has been committed in the south for many years, but when the last presidential election took place, practically every colored boy and girl in America was for Warren G. Harding as president. Why did we want you? The answer was: He is a Republican and will stop that terrible crime - lynching. You were elected, but now and then there could be heard of a few lynchings. Mr. President, why do they lynch the Negro? Has not he done his full share or bit in the making of this new land? When America was fighting for independence, was not Crispus Attucks, a negro, the first man killed? There are many others that could be named, but time and space will not permit me. When the trumpet was blown for civil strife, did not the Negro give his life as well as the Anglo-Saxon? During the world war, Negro boys also sacrificed their lives as well, and as bravely as the white man, that democracy might rule the earth. This reminds me of our glorious song "My Country 'tis of Thee, Sweet land of Liberty." Mr. President, you are aware of the fact that we have not our full liberty but still we sing the song by faith in the future.   ABP

I admit that there are some lawless Negroes in America, as well as whites, capable of committing horrible crimes. All people are not as good as others, but, Mr. President, what good does lynching do? One man may be lynched for a crime of which another has committed. It does not tend to make a nation better, it only brings race prejudice and hatred. What good or use is the law, if the lynchers are going to put the law in their own hands. Mr. President, imagine yourself about to be lynched for something of which you know nothing about. Men sieze you from some place of refuge, carry you to the heart of the town, place a rope around you and burn you, while men, women and children are jeering amidst all your pain and agony. It is enough to make one ashamed not to use his full influence against this horrible crime.

A bill has been introduced in Congress by Representative Dyer a Republican) to prevent lynching, or make it a criminal offense. Mr. President, it is incumbent upon you, the chief executive of all Americans to urge the passage of this bill. If lynching is permitted in the south, finally it will spread to the north, doing nothing but kindling the flames of racial and personal hatred, and sowing the seeds of internal strife. There are some courageous and conscientious senators who are in favor of the passage of the bill, but, Mr. President, we are looking to

Document 26a. Letter to Warren G. Harding from Ara Lee Settle, June 18, 1922. [National Archives]

you to see it through.   If this country had more men such as Mr. Dyer it would be "Sweet land of Liberty".

One might say, push the bill away until a more opportune time presents itself when they would be more able to debate on it.   But as a well known man has said, "Today is the only real day promised" Why not do that today and hurl lynching into a bottomless pit to remain forever? Mr. President, we are looking and pleading to you.

During the war the colored people were very patriotic, they bought Liberty Bonds, War Saving Stamps, Thrift Stamps, had meatless, sugarless, wheatless days, also they crocheted, knitted and embroideried for the boys over there while they were fighting for "dear old America", but mind you some of the same Colored boys have since returned to America and have been lynched in a way that has been heretofore explained.

When lynching has been expurged, then we may all sing from our hearts with a true meaning:
> "My Country 'tis of thee,
> Sweet land of Liberty,
> Of thee I Sing.
> Land where my fathers died,
> Land of the Pilgrims pride,
> Frome every mountain side,
> Let Freeomd ring.

Once more, Mr. Harding, we are looking to you, to you, to you.

Respectfully yours,

Ara Lee Settle. Section 6

17 years of age.

2636 Nichols ave. S. E. (Home address)

Copperhill, Tennessee.
November 21, 1928.

Mrs. Mable Walker Willebrandt
Washington, D. C.

My dear Mrs. Willebrandt:

Do you think prohibition would be more efficiently enforced under the Department of Justice or under the Secretary of Treasury as it has been here to fore?

I am a student in the high school in my home town. One of my teachers suprised the students and patrons a short time ago by saying prohibition had never been enforced and will never be enforced. He stated that it is very unpopular. He made other remarks detrimental to the students. I favor prohibition and would value your opinion as to the best method of enforcement.

Personally, I wish to say you are due much creat for loyal service during the recent presidential campaign. We are Hoover democrats.

Very sincerely yours,
(miss) Gladys W. Center

Document 27. Letter to Mrs. Mable Walker Willebrandt from Gladys W. Center, November 21, 1928. [National Archives]

218 - W. Canton St.
Boston, Mass.
November 20, 1929.

Mr. Herbert Hoover, President
of the United States of America

Dear Sir:

I, a negro of twenty years, have just learned of another lynching of a member of my Race, which took place in Florida a few days ago. Although I dislike to bother you Sir, I am compelled to appeal to you to stop lynching in the United States of any man, regardless of race or color. I feel that you, as President of this nation, are better able to stop this outrage, than any other person.

Are the members of my Race and I, to be murdered and hacked by other Americans whose faces are white, but whose souls are of the blackest? Are we, who after having suffered numerous insults at the hands of the white race, who have, nevertheless, fought and died for the Red, White and Blue

to be continually restricted of
natural rights?

Sir, I see only one way
which will end lynching.
That is, for the President
of the nation to take an
active part against those
states of the Union that allow
such atrocious crimes.

Sir, do you think that
because a woman of your Race
is attacked by a man of my
Race that this man should be
put to death without even
having a trial? Is not the
woman's life as seriously endangered
whether it be a white or a black
man?

Of course, I believe that any man
who commits such a crime should
be given, at least a life sentence
at hard labor, but I do not
think he should be killed by
a lawless, blood-thirsty gang.

Document 28b. Letter to Mr. Herbert Hoover, President, from
Horace Robinson, November 20, 1929. [National Archives]

Sir, I appeal to you, I beg of you to protect my Race, who after all, are citizens of America as well as the white Race.

Sir, do you think that I would leave a white person in water where that person is struggling for his life, when I know that I can save him? No, Sir. I would not. For I would realize that although he is not a member of my Race, he is a human being, therefore he deserves to be saved.

Sir, I trust you will pardon me for taking up some of your valuable time, but I felt that I would be unable to do any constructive thinking until I had made an appeal to you on behalf of my race and me.

Respectfully yours
Horace Robinson

Document 28c. Letter to Mr. Herbert Hoover, President, from
Horace Robinson, November 20, 1929. [National Archives]

Excerpts from a Questionaire Relative to Moral Problems in the High Schools as judged by the students, North Central Association of Colleges and Schools, covering 19 States. Edited by Prof.C.O. Davis, University of Michigan, Ann Arbor, Michigan.

The chief moral qualities exhibited by pupils:
Honesty 30%
Fellowship 12%
Clean habits 19%
Courtesy lowest with only 9%

The most regretable practices of boys in school:
Smoking 38%
Swearing 19%
Drinking 8%
Telling vulgar stories 5%

The most regretable practices of girls in school:
Cosmetics 17%
Flirting & petting 14%
Profane language 12%

Factors tending to develope high moral qualities among pupils:
Teacher 31%
School Organization 18%
Athletics 17%

Invidious factors tending to undermine right conduct:
Certain low minded people 63%
Poor discipline 11%
Immoral parties 11%

How could school help to develope morality among pupils?
Course in morals 32%
Stricter Rules 21%
Talks 19%

Is a course in moral education desirable?
61% of replies said "Yes",
39% of replies said "No".

Some forces which are the most helpful:
Mother 20%
Father 17%
Teacher 11%

Influences which made pupils do what they should not have done:
Evil companions 55%
Personal weakness 10%
Immoral movies 9%
Wish to be popular & desire for a good time 6%.

Highest school ambitions:
To be all around capable person 62%
Excellent student 31%

Things pupils are proud of:
The High School spirit 22%
Athletic Activities 20%
Moral strength 12%

What change in class procedure advocated?
More class discussions 23%
More recitations by pupils 20%
More explanations 23%

Things making a boy popular:
Athletics 21%
Scholarship 14%
Good looks 10%
Dependability has 1%
Capability only 2%
Character only 2% & takes 12th place of 18 questions asked.

Things that make a girl popular:
Appearance 17%
Scholarship 13%
Personality 9%
Morality 4%
Character only 3% & takes 15th place of 18 questions asked.

What would you expect to learn fr. a course in marriage, home & parenthood?
How to make married life a success 36%
Sex instruction (what it is all about) 21%
Parenthood 19%

Characteristics of an ideal boy:
Education 10%
Good morals 10%
Athletics 10%

Characteristics of an ideal girl:
Honesty 10%
Education 10%
Good looks 9%
Morality 5%
Capability 3%

Present causes of worry:
Choice of vocation 27%
Money matters 21%
Studies 16%
Religious matters 2%(lowest of ten questions).

Future life problems:
Marriage 19%
Money 19%
Vocation 17%
Service 4%

Admission from pupils of using vulgar or profane language:
Yes 31%, No. 69%.

Flying into fits of violent temper:
Yes 27%, No. 73%
Telling or willingly listening to vulgar stories: Yes 34%, No.66%.

Note: That a goodly number of pupils regret the fact that the full meaning of life is not made clear to them by the school.

Pathfinders of America, Human Engineers,
311 Lincoln Bldg., Detroit, Mich.

198589

Chas. D. Levy
WHOLESALE DRY GOODS
OFFICES AND SALESROOMS
1444 ~ 1450 St. Clair Avenue
CLEVELAND OHIO
June 24th, 1924.

Honorable Calvin Coolidge,
        President of the United States,
            Washington, D. C.

My Dear Mr. President:

        I have been a staunch Republican for many
years, casting my first vote for James A. Garfield.

        I have twenty-three Department Stores lo-
cated throughout the different towns and cities of Ohio.
In some of these towns and cities the Ku Klux Klan organization has placed a boycott on several of my stores, on
account of me being fortunate enough to be born a Hebrew,
and just as soon as the present leases expire I will be
compelled to move from these sections.

        In the town of Ashland, Ohio, where one of my
stores is located, there was held a meeting in the Public
Square, and in front of thousands of spectators who had
gathered to hear the speakers, the Ku Klux Klan openly
told the audience they should not patronize any Jewish
merchant. I think this is just plain boycott and very un-
fair to an American citizen or even a Non-American citizen.

        I have read your platform and taken special
notice to the paragraph in which you state that you demand
"law and order" and "the protection of all citizens."

        All I am asking for is your protection in this
matter. If you have promised it for the next four years
there is no reason why you cannot give it to us now, as you
are The President now, of this glorious country, the same
as I hope you will be for the next four years.

        I await your kind reply for which I thank you
in advance.

                        Very sincerely,

CDL/N

Document 30. Letter to the Hon. Calvin Coolidge from Charles D. Levy, June 24, 1924. [National Archives]

THE
KU KLUX KLAN

Invites You to the Portals of the

INVISIBLE EMPIRE

1. **You must** be born in the U. S. A.

2. **You must** swear unqualified allegiance to the **GOVERNMENT** of the **UNITED STATES** of **AMERICA**, its **CONSTI= TUTION**, and its **FLAG**, above any other and every kind of government, civil, political, or ecclesiastical in the whole world.

3. **YOU MUST** believe in the tenants of the **CHRISTIAN** religion and owe no allegiance of any degree or nature to any foreign govern- ment, nation, political institution, sect, people, or person.

4. **YOU MUST** believe in **WHITE** supremacy.

If you measure up to requirements you may join. Further information will be mailed to you upon request---your name, address, and tele- phone number will be held secret and sacred when placed upon reverse side and mailed to

P. O. BOX No. 3, WALBROOK STATION P. O.
BALTIMORE, MD.

198589 — 483

Document 31. Flyer, "The Ku Klux Klan Invites You to the Portals . . .," n.d. [National Archives]

Justice 28 ..st Pearl St., 198589

New Haven, Connecticut.

September 24th, 1921.

RECORDED

198589 - 219

Hon. Warren G. Harding, President,

Washington, D.C.

Dear President Harding;-

I hope that you may pardon the liberty I am taking of addressing you and that you may be able to find a spare moment in which to read this letter;

I do not know that you are at all interested in the subject, yet our daily papers intimate that you are.

I have reference to that organization known as the Ku Klux Klan.

While I may not be a member of it at the same time so much is being published that it has naturally aroused my interest. Some say that you are going to call upon it to disband because it is un-American.

I cannot understand why it is un-American because a large group of our citizens who are native born and of the Protestant faith want to have a society of their own, just as those of other creeds and national-ities. I am an American of the 10th generation and rather resent the inference that I am un-American because I see no harm in it.

Neither do I see why it should not have its own regalia if it so elects and uses it properly. Yet the press is assailing it at every turn. I am for Law and Order first, last and all the time. I believe in fair play. This whole thing has so worked upon me that I cannot help addressing MY President so that he may know my feelings, and at the same time ask that if there is an investigation in which he may have his part that he will see to it that we are fully informed as regards the outcome.

With deep esteem and respect, Mr. President, believe me

Very sincerely

Arthur James Mann

Ackd 10/12/21

Document 32. Letter to Warren G. Harding from Arthur James Mann, September 24, 1921. [National Archives]

Document 33. Photograph, "KKK women marching," Washington, DC, 1928. [National Archives]

198589

Attorney General Sargeant
National Capitol
Washington, D. C.

198589-667

5
MAI   MAR 15 1928

Dear Sir:

Eighteen months ago a mob
under guise of the K.K.K. attacked
and drove my father from (his bed)
his dwelling, about midnight. due to
terror a very young brother of mine
was forced to flee from the house, from
whence he went to a nearly plowed field
where he buried himself in a deep furrow.
Out of fear for his life, my father, dressed
in a very thin night gown, escaped to
a nearby copse where he spent most of
the night in a drizzle. After the effort
of the felons to get my father was foiled
they battered down a door against which
my mother and sister franticly pushed to
stay them; they riddled another door with
bullets.

Sir, Russia with her flowing blood and
Sovietism has little more than surpassed

this dastardly outrage upon peace and life.

We, the Burdick family, haven't sufficient money to investigate thoroughly and prosecute, that is bring these curs to justice. Through the months that have passed, since this occurrence, my father has thru discretion seen it necessary to go well armed; he has found that he has had to do much that the state should have done, that is guard his life. We, my father and I, are tax payers and citizens of the United States. Since the county and the state have failed to act upon this constitutional offense I supplicate you in the name of peace, liberty, happiness, and life to see that action is had.

My father and his family reside at Ethridge, Tenn. (G. U. Burdick)

Very sincerely yours,
Rampy J. Burdick

Document 35. Photograph, "President Calvin Coolidge," n.d. [National Archives]

W. E. Ryan,
Fontanet Courts,
1400 Fairmont St., N.W.

Washington, D. C.
July 28, 1924

Honorable Calvin Cooledge,
President of the United States,

Mr. President:

Enclosed please find an Editorial
Clipping, Washington Post, even date.

Mr. President, has not the hour struck
when the Federal Government should at least call
the attention of the Governors of the States of
the United States, to these reported outrages, law
violations, etc. etc., as are mentioned in the
enclosed Editorial Clipping!

The eyes of all true Americans and those
of the peoples of the civilized world are upon an
invisible, masked, association of men (and women
too now,) who are forcing its, or their, unlawful
will upon other American citizens.

I am the son of a Union Soldier, who died
for his and our country!   I am also the father of
an only son, who is a World-War veteran.

Did my father die, and my son serve as a
World-War soldier for the freedom of man but to
permit now, an Unamerican Association of men and
women to openly, but masked, violate our laws! Is
it not time for the Executive, through the Attorney
General of the United States to act!

Very truly yours,

WER:HH

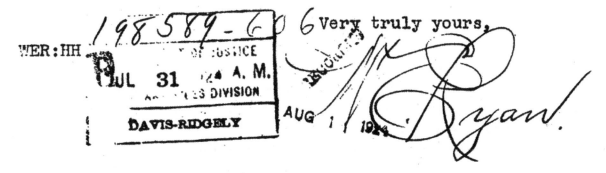

The Washington Post.

TERMS OF SUBSCRIPTION
Payable in Advance

Delivered by Carrier in Washington and Alexandria

Daily, Sunday included, one year.......................$8.40
Daily, Sunday excepted, one year....................... 6.00
Sunday only, one year................................... 2.40
Daily, Sunday included, one month...................... .70
Daily, Sunday excepted, one month..................... .50
Sunday only, one month................................ .20

By Mail, Postage Prepaid

Daily and Sunday	Sunday Only	Daily Only
One year....$10.00	One year......$3.00	One year....$7.00
Six months.. 5.00	Six months..... 1.50	Six months... 3.50
One month.. .85	One month..... .25	One month... .60

All Subscriptions by Mail Payable in Advance

New subscriptions for The Post or renewals will not be accepted unless payment accompanies the order. Remittances should be made by drafts, checks, postoffice orders, registered letters or express orders, payable to

THE WASHINGTON POST CO.
Washington, D. C.
EDWARD B. McLEAN, President and Publisher
GEORGE HARVEY, Editor

Entered at the Postoffice at Washington, D. C., as second-class mail matter.

Foreign Advertising Representatives—PAUL BLOCK, Park avenue and Forty-sixth street, New York; Century Building, Chicago; Little Building, Boston; 1311 Kresge Building, Detroit.

Monday, July 28, 1924.

RESPONSIBILITY.

The other day a victim of lawlessness was tarred and feathered and branded with "K. K. K." A short time before that a woman in New Jersey was driven to sacrifice her home by reported "K. K. K." agents. Before that a citizen of Virginia was terrorized by a band claiming to be of the klan and driven into exile.

The official "K. K. K." disclaims these manifestations of violence, or rather threatened violence, and the disclaimer may be technically accurate. But the "K. K. K." can not disclaim responsibility for such violence in spirit and in reality. It is the hooded order that has set the fashion in lawlessness and in arbitrary attacks upon others. It has donned the robe and the mask, and it is at least indirectly responsible for those who imitate it for unlawful purposes. They have set the example and they are responsible for the results.

ISAAC McCLELLAN
SHERIDAN

CIRCUIT COURT THIRD MONDAYS IN
FEBRUARY AND AUGUST
CHANCERY COURT EACH MONTH

JNO. L. McCLELLAN
MALVERN

COUNTY COURT FIRST MONDAYS IN
JANUARY, APRIL, JULY AND OCTOBER
PROBATE COURT THIRD MONDAYS IN
JANUARY, APRIL, JULY AND OCTOBER

McCLELLAN & McCLELLAN

ATTORNEYS-AT-LAW

SHERIDAN, ARKANSAS

Feb. 10th, 1923

Department of Justice,

Washington, D. C.

My Dear Sir:-

I see in the papers that the Department of Justice is to send out detectives etc and see if the mobs and other intimidations are being directed by the K.K.K's and I want to say a little about things in Arkansas.

They are so thoroughly organized here, that the courts, and principal officials are members, and when they want a jury, they summons no one but their own, and if a K.K.K. is in any way involved in a suit, all of them are aiders and abettors, and an anti stands no chance at all in court against one of the members. It makes no difference what the evidence is or what the law is, the member wins. This sentiment is also to some extent getting into churches and in all walks of society, and in our public schools as to directors and teachers.

Several people here have received letters from them in a threatening manner, and it is not the low down or criminal class altogether, but some of the best citizens of our community who do not agree with the acts of this organization, have received letters. Some of them are now gone, as they felt like they had no protection. Many others are talking of selling out and leaving if they only knew where to go.

There is going to have to be something done as the State authorities cannot meet it, because when they go to a place to organize they try to get all the officials and preachers in to start the organization. If the Federal Government cannot meet the issue at once and successfully, the election of 1924 will witness the downfall of our Republic I fear. This matter is too big for partisanship, so all Americans should gladly unite now to fight the common enemy of our liberties. Shall the government endure or shall the Invisible Empire succeed it? Push your investigations at once and fast before it is too late.

Yours very truly,

Isaac McClellan

Document 37. Letter to Department of Justice from Isaac McClellan, February 10, 1923. [National Archives]

Selma,Ala Dec,5,24,

U,S DIST ATTY Stone

Washington

Dear Sir,   D,C,

I wish to call your attention to the Klu ,Lk Klan

Which has been organised here here recentlythey are trying

to run this sectionthey are running negros awayand if

ane klan has a greivence against them or any one

they warn them to leave or they will take them out and giv

them a flogginthey have about 1ooo members here and

there their hall is over W,R R city Ticket OfficeIn

The Gillman BuildingThey meet there every Thursday night

And they gets Difrent Persons up there before themAnd they

handle them Very RuffThey had L,C.Farley ManagerUp There And gav

Gave him 2 Weeks To leaveAnd He LeftAS you well Know Farley Co

Is a eastern Company They had Mr Merry Walker s Son up Before

Them andHandled him Very ruffalso Had a negro named Shannon W

Who lived on Harry Smith Place to leave inA weekAnd Smith

went to the ring leadersand resented about renning his ne

negro tennants,most of The state and Officials Belong to thi

Klan ang one who does not belongto it has a poor showing

And the onlyShowing a person is to appeal to the U,S atty, T

Go have The Us Grand jury to investigateThese thingsAs i

Give ,you a few whoo came undermy personal knolledge

the ring leaders of the klans herearrPhillip Shanks,

Ed Keoble Dr Frank Jones DR RenyoldsDr Thomas Drummond G

Gains Mack strong, Dr ChristenberyRoscoe Hinson

Document 38a. Letter to U.S. District Attorney [Harlan F.] Stone
from S. Jonce, December 5, 1924. [National Archives]

EM... E,M,McDaniels Charlie JonesThey arec also fighting the Jews a

And The Catholic And Putting on A boy cot against these people

Any Clas or Band of menWho can Run This sectionRegard to the rig

hts of the mases of people makes this country un safe for peopl

e to live in and it takeshis rights of freedom awayAnd if

it continues to go on no telling where it willgo as a few willr

ruleand people will have to doand vote as the klan ordersn

     Wish you would have this matterd investigated whe

the next grand jury nmeets and see if this affair does not go s

so far as to take the rights and libberty of anamerican citz

en,

        S,yours Truly

          S,Jonce,

Document 38b. Letter to U.S. District Attorney [Harlan F.] Stone
from S. Jonce, December 5, 1924. [National Archives]

Document 39. Photograph, "Charles A. Lindbergh loading cargo," Lambert Field, St. Louis, 1925. [National Archives]

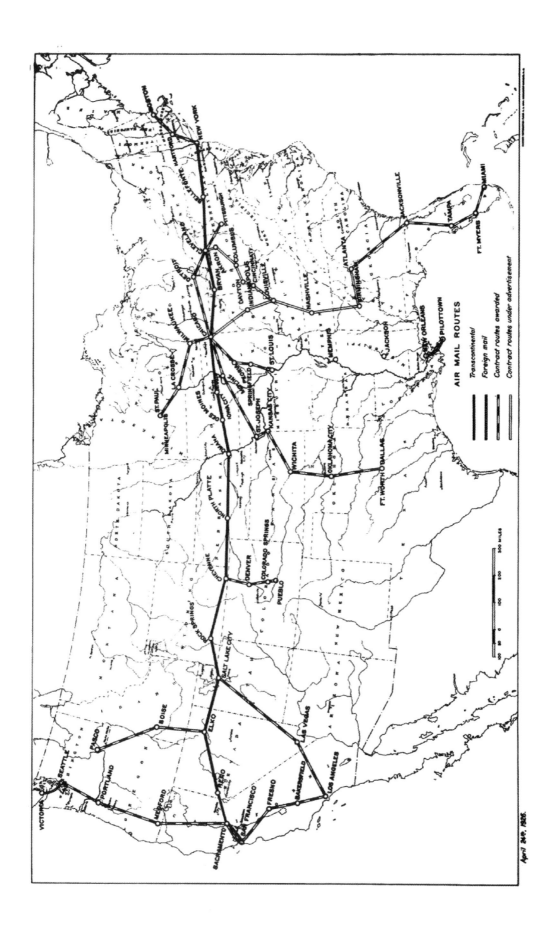

Document 40. Post Office Department map of airmail routes, April 24, 1926. [National Archives]

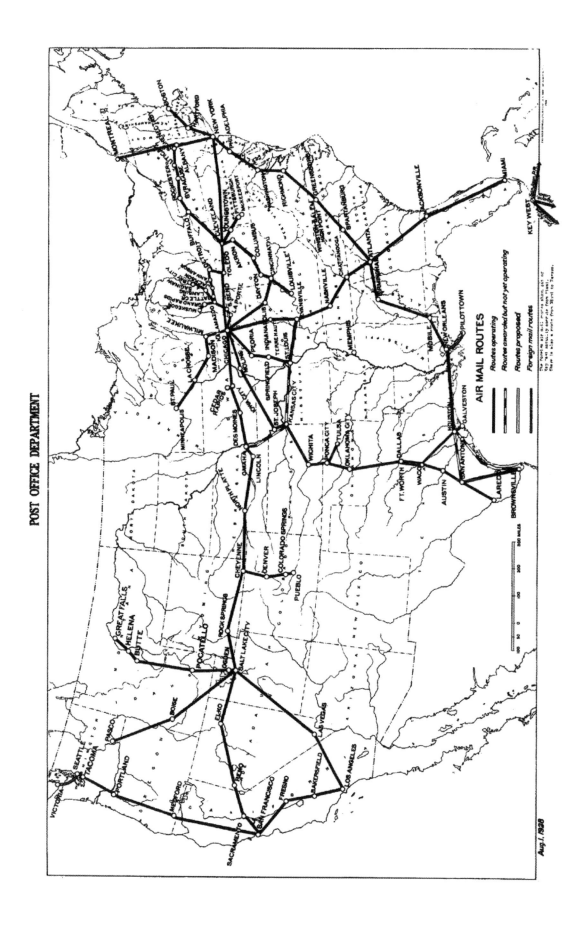

POST OFFICE DEPARTMENT

AIR MAIL ROUTES

Routes operating
Routes awarded but not yet operating
Routes proposed
Foreign mail routes

Aug. 1, 1928.

Document 41. Post Office Department map of airmail routes, August 1, 1928. [National Archives]

TAKING THE WORK OUT OF WASHING

WITH A

"1900 Cataract" Electric Washer

Here Are Some of the Things the "Cataract" Will Do for You

You Hire a Laundress—It will enable her to do your work in less than half the usual time. Time enough left to do the ironing the same day. Or work that usually requires two days can be done in one. A net saving of one day—$2.50 per week—$130.00 per year.

Besides this Saving—You can have an abundance of clean linen—always fresh—always ready for instant use—preserving its good looks indefinitely.

If You Do It Yourself—Again saves half the time—all the rubbing—all the wringing—hence all the hard work.

Surely things that are worth while.

The "Cataract" is Guaranteed Against Defects in Material or Workmanship

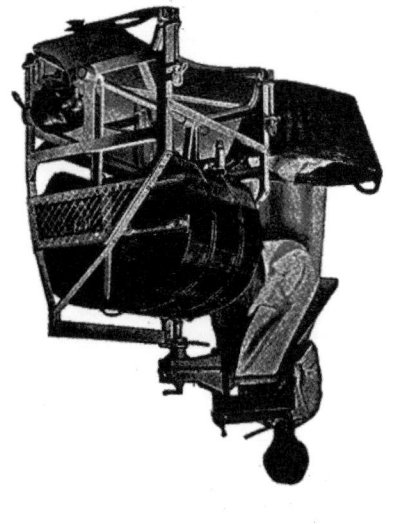

The Wringer Is Reversible and Easily Swung to Any Position Desired. You Can Wring and Wash at the Same Time.

No Cylinder to Lift Out for Cleaning After Each Washing. Note in the Figure Eight Movement How the Cataract Forces the Water and Suds Over, Under and Through the Clothes Instead of Rubbing the Life Out of Them.

THE worst part of the housework is the washing, when done in the old way on the rub-board, rasping the dirt and soil out of each piece separately, by hand. If you have a hand machine it will help out, but even then some one must push and pull the handle back and forth, and although it is not hard, it becomes arduous before the family washing is completed. Then the wringer must be turned by hand and this is by far more tiresome than operating the washer.

Hand operated machines have been done away with in the factory, in the office and in the institution and in fact, everywhere. Men now use machinery operated by power. Why should women not do likewise?

The "1900" Cataract Washer is so simple in design and construction that no knowledge of machinery or electricity is necessary to produce work of the finest quality. You simply follow our brief instructions for its proper use.

Costs 1 to 2 Cents for Electricity to Do the Family Wash

Our Special Offer on the Cataract
Our liberal offer of monthly payments will make you the owner of this wonderful Electric Washing Machine and Wringer.

THE following comparison, adopted from *Good Housekeeping*, gives an impartial idea of the cost of the new and the old method of washing:

Electric Washer (approximate cost).$175.00
  Operating cost (1 year)......... 2.50
  Interest on investment (6 per cent. for 1 year)................. 10.50

Total cost....................$188.00

The Electric Washer if sold at the end of one year for one-half its cost......................... 94.00

Leaves the actual cost for one year.. $94.00

A laundress costs—
  In wages $3.00 per day, or......$156.00 per year
  In food and car fare, 50c. per day, or......................... 26.00 per year

Total cost per year............$182.00

Comparison:
  Laundress per year............$182.00
  Electric Washer 94.00

Balance in favor of machine....... $88.00

This does not take into consideration the cost of soap or other incidentals, as they are about the same in both cases.

If you choose to do the work yourself, the Electric Washer will save the entire amount usually paid the laundress, and in five years will save many times its cost.

Simple in Design—Easy to Operate

THE GRAND PRIZE
"1900 CATARACT" WASHER
MADE IN TWO SIZES
FAMILY SIZE AND LAUNDRY SIZE

"SHE SITS AND SEWS WHILE THE WASHER GOES"

SPECIFICATIONS AND DATA

TYPE—Oscillating Tub—Figure 8 movement of water.

Power transmitted from motor mounted on swinging base—under spring tension—by flat endless belt.

Reversible Wringer—shaft driven—adjustable to all required positions for use in connection with two washtubs.

CONSTRUCTION—Frame—extra heavy—all metal—mounted on casters with 4 adjustable lifting levers.

Tub—solid copper—Detachable cover.

Wringer—Rock Maple Frame—extra quality white rubber rolls—all cog wheels enclosed. Equipped with safety release attachment.

Fast moving parts of driving mechanism fully enclosed running in oil.

	SIZE	
	FAMILY	LAUNDRY
Capacity of Tub—Equivalent of...	8 bed sheets	12 bed sheets
Output per hour " " ...	40 " "	60 " "
Motor—Highest Standard of Quality—Special Design.		
Wringer—Dimension of Rolls...	11" x 1¾"	12" x 1¾"
Electric Current—Estimated cost per hour...	2 Cents	2½ Cents
Actual Floor Space (overall) required...	35½" x 28½"	39½" x 28½"
Weight { Gross shipping...	350 lbs.	377 lbs.
{ Net...	272 "	290 "

THE "1900" WASHER COMPANY
BINGHAMTON, N. Y.

Make It Yourself

BREW YOUR OWN BEER
AT HOME WITH

Picture to yourself a glassful of Healthful, Zestful, Invigorating Beer that tops the glass with a rich creamy foam. Sounds good, doesn't it? Well, make it yourself with **BRUMALT** and you will have all the beer you want whenever you want it, at less than a cent a glass. Our instructions are simple and it is very easy to make the finest beer with **BRUMALT**.

EACH
2½ LB.
CAN
MAKES 58
BOTTLES
OF
THE
FINEST
BEER

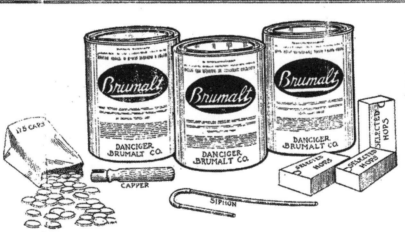

EACH
2½ LB.
CAN
MAKES 58
BOTTLES
OF
THE
FINEST
BEER

Brumalt is a Pure and Highly Concentrated Extract of Pure Barley Malt Specially Prepared for Beverage Purposes. Only by using Brumalt are you assured of getting a pure healthful, invigorating Beer.

SEND US YOUR ORDER TODAY

Danciger Brumalt Company

306-08-10 West Sixth St.   **KANSAS CITY, MO**

The Diocesan Bureau of Social Service

INCORPORATED

Central Office

244 Main Street, Hartford, Connecticut

TELEPHONE. 2-2857

RT. REV. JOHN J. NILAN, D. D.
PRESIDENT

REV. MATTHEW J. JUDGE
DIOCESAN DIRECTOR

MISS MARGUERITE BOYLAN, A. M.
EXECUTIVE SECRETARY

DISTRICT OFFICES

BRIDGEPORT
CATHOLIC CHARITABLE BUREAU
224 WASHINGTON AVENUE

NEW HAVEN
CATHOLIC SOCIAL SERVICE BUREAU
478 ORANGE STREET

NEW LONDON
42 JAY STREET

WATERBURY
29 FIELD STREET

February 4, 1924.

Hon. George P. McLean,
United States Senator,
Washingtonm D.C.
My dear Mr. McLean:

      We, the Legislative Committee of the Connecticut Council
of Catholoc Women, in meeting assembled this fourth day of February,
1924, represetning ten thousand individual members and sixty affiliated
organizations, hereby enter our protest against the measure known as
the Equal Rights Amendment.

      This measure is sponsored by the National Women's Party,
the only group of women to our knowledged interested in its passage.
Our interest in the nearly twelve millon women employed in industry
today, prompts this protest. It has taken years to obtain legislation
which will offer the right protection to women workers, limitations
of hours, prohibition of night work, mothers compensations, etc.

      With the passage of this measure all of this legislation
will be invalidated unless there is similiar legislation for men.

      Can we forget the women are physiologically different from men?
That they have maternal functions to perform and for the good of the
future citizens the mothers and potential mothers Have had such
legislation for them sustained by the courts.

      After a serious consideration of this measure we trust you
will appreciate our stand.

      We look to you to see that the inters of our women workers
is not jeopardized.

Sincerely yours,
Legislative Committee.
Connecticut Council of Catholic. Women.

Jane D. Mahoney, Norwich, Ct
Rosemary Brady, Meriden, Conn
Margaret Elliott, Torrington
Mrs. Margaret C. Squires, Willimantic
Mary E. Kennelly, Middletown Ct.
Eleanor H. Reilly, Willimantic Ct.
Mary S. Barrett, Windsor Locks.
Mae Egan, Windsor Locks
Mae V. tetell, Thompsonville Conn.

Mary P. O'Flaherty
Mrs. Mary Belanger, Hartford Ct.
(Mrs) Agnes M. Lynn, Hartford.
Marguerite T. Boylan, Hartford Conn.

Document 45. Letter to Hon. George P. McLean from Legislative Committee,
Connecticut Council of Catholic Women, February 4, 1924. [National Archives]

H. J. RES. 75

IN THE HOUSE OF REPRESENTATIVES.

DECEMBER 13, 1923.

Mr. ANTHONY introduced the following joint resolution; which was referred to the Committee on the Judiciary and ordered to be printed.

JOINT RESOLUTION

Proposing an amendment to the Constitution of the United States.

1 *Resolved by the Senate and House of Representatives*

2 *of the United States of America in Congress assembled*

3 *(two-thirds of each House concurring therein),* That the

4 following article is proposed as an amendment to the Con-

5 stitution of the United States which shall be valid, to all

6 intents and purposes, as part of the Constitution when

7 ratified by the legislatures of three-fourths of the several

8 States:

9 ARTICLE XX.

10 "Men an women shall have equal rights throughout

11 the United States and every place subject to its jurisdiction.

12 "Congress shall have power to enforce this article by

13 appropriate legislation."

Document 46. House Joint Resolution 75, 68th Congress, 1st session, December 13, 1923. [National Archives]

1. PROPORTION OF MALES AND FEMALES 10 YEARS OF AGE AND OVER ENGAGED IN EACH GENERAL DIVISION OF GAINFUL OCCUPATIONS: 1920.

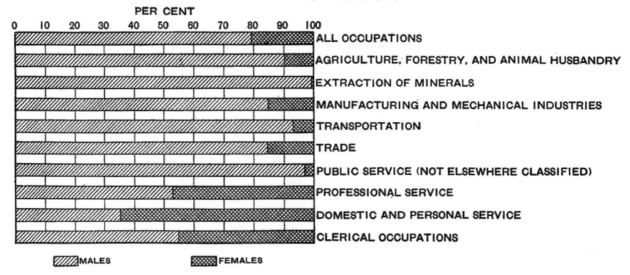

2. PROPORTION WHICH GAINFUL WORKERS OF BOTH SEXES, IN EACH SPECIFIED AGE GROUP, CONSTITUTED OF ALL GAINFUL WORKERS, AND THE PROPORTION WHICH MALES AND FEMALES OF EACH AGE GROUP FORMED OF TOTAL MALE AND FEMALE WORKERS: 1920.

3. PROPORTION OF EACH PRINCIPAL CLASS OF POPULATION 10 YEARS OF AGE AND OVER, BOTH SEXES, MALES AND FEMALES, ENGAGED IN GAINFUL OCCUPATIONS: 1920.

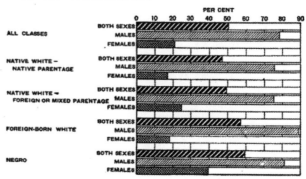

5. PROPORTION OF MARRIED AND OF SINGLE, WIDOWED, DIVORCED, AND UNKNOWN WOMEN AMONG WOMEN 15 YEARS OF AGE AND OVER IN EACH GENERAL DIVISION OF GAINFUL OCCUPATIONS: 1920.

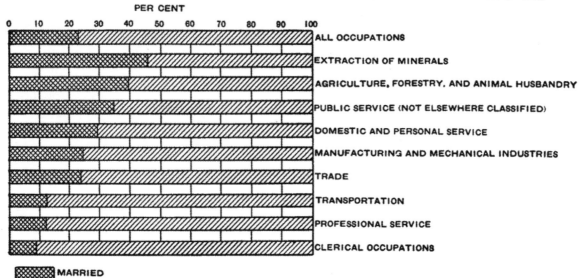

Document 47. Charts relating to the employment of men and women, *Statistical Atlas of the United States*, 1924, p. 256 and 267. [National Archives]

Document 48. Photograph, "Telephone operators," April 7, 1927. [National Archives]

Make housewives stop, look and think about the "Universal" Washer. Keep them thinking and you'll prepare them for buying. Dress your window with the "Universal" Washer and this Nine-Piece Window Trim— a great combination to attract attention, hold interest and start women thinking "Universal."

Set No. W99

Document 49. Suggested window display from *Help for the Dealer*, Landers, Frary and Clark, New Britain, CT, n.d. [National Archives]

J.O. WELLS, President.   J. G. CARVER, Vice Prest.   G.B. PAXTON, Secy & Treas.

ESTABLISHED 1879 – INCORPORATED 1889.

COOPER, WELLS & CO.

Capital Stock $500,000.

ST. JOSEPH, MICH.
April 20, 1923.

Hon. James A. Davis,
Secretary of Labor,
Washington, D. C.

Dear Sir:-

Our attention has been called to a letter you have written to President Harding in regard to the labor situation.

We would like to take issue with you in regard to the present
immigration law not effecting the labor situation, for in our
opinion it is very seriously effecting it.

We have been operating a hosiery mill at this point for forty-
five years, and as Berrien County is largely settled by Germans
and Russians, we have always had quite an influx through immigration every year until the past two or three years. We
thought when the War was over that our labor troubles would
soon be a thing of the past.   But just when things were beginning to improve the Three Percent Immigration Law was passed,
and as a result very little immigration is coming to this point.

In 1920, to help solve our labor difficulties, we built a dormitory for girls where they can live at a cost of $5.00 a week
for room and board.   Even this we are unable to keep filled
and at present have room for from fifteen to twenty additional
girls.

We recently tried to get some girls from Gary, Indiana, and
had the Rev. Zindler of this city write to a friend of his in
that city, and we are enclosing his letter, which you will notice
also blames the present immigration law for the labor shortage.

We do not believe all restrictions should be taken off immigration, but we believe that the restriction should be qualita-
tive and not quantitative.   The class of immigrants that have in
the past come to this locality, have always been high grade.
The greater part of the best farms in Berrien County are owned
by people of German and Russian descent, and we believe it is a
great injustice not to permit the right kind of immigrants to
land in this country simply because their quota of three percent

Enclosd literature kept CC

Document 50a. Letter to the Hon. James A. Davis from J. O. Wells, April 20, 1923. [National Archives]

Hon. James A. Davis.

happens to be filled — especially at a time when the country needs common labor as it never has before.

We can all see the old vicious circle started — wages being increased throughout the country — prices on commodities going up. Then another circle of wage increases, then another advance in commodities until we will again have a buyers strike such as we had in 1920.

We are enclosing some circulars of our Lakeside Dormitory and sending you one of our booklets under separate cover. We believe you will agree with us that we are doing everything in our power to secure help.

Yours truly,

COOPER WELLS & COMPANY,

JOW:JR

J. O. Wells   Pres.

More Stranded Girls than Ever

Defeat and Disillusionment Along the City's Gay White Way Still the Lot of the Modern Girl, Despite Her Self-Reliance; but She Is Better Able to Emerge Safely from Her Predicament than the Girl of Yesterday

Modern girls view the metropolis with much more confidence and equanimity than did country girls of a generation ago, but even these self-sufficient young women often go broke before they secure a job and their first pay envelope.

EVERY girl who comes to New York should have at least enough money to last for three or four weeks, figuring at the rate of about $25 to $30 a week. Girls must count on paying at least $7 or $8 a week for a room, and this is the very lowest figure for which a self-respecting girl can secure respectable lodgings. She must figure on about $10 a week for food, several dollars for laundry and several more for carfare, telephone calls and other incidentals. Many girls arrive in New York with less than $25.

DR. A. M. YOUNG,
Secretary of the Memorial Committee, Volunteers of America.

Maude Ballington Booth, wife of the founder of the Volunteers of America and co-worker with her husband in organized relief work.

Despite her capabilities, the girl of today is likely to find job-hunting in New York City a long, heart-breaking struggle, because competition is so great.

(Copyright, 1929.)

General Ballington Booth, founder of the Volunteers of America. This organization is raising funds to erect a home for stranded girls in New York City as a memorial to General and Mrs. Booth's many years of philanthropic service.

BY CAROL BIRD

THOUSANDS of women and girls from all parts of the country drift into New York City as part of the ambitious army of more than two hundred thousand which each year enters the mecca of fame and fortune. A larger percentage of them than ever before are becoming stranded, meeting defeat and disillusionment, despite the much-vaunted efficiency and independence of the modern girl.

Broke, hungry, their clothes gone shabby from days of job-hunting, without even the fare to go back to the farm or the towns whence they came, they are up against a disheartening and altogether terrifying problem.

"Never before in history has woman reached the pinnacle of self-assurance and independence on which she stands today; yet the financial situation has not altered in the least, and if a girl comes to New York without money to bridge the gap between her arrival and her securing of a job and a pay envelope, she is in the same predicament as was her less able sister of several decades ago," said Dr. A. M. Young, secretary of the memorial committee of the Volunteers of America, which is now raising funds for a home for stranded women and girls, to be an anniversary foundation dedicated to General Ballington Booth and his wife, commemorating their 50 years of philanthropic service.

"HERE in New York one finds culture, educational opportunities, fascinating social life, wealth, chances for eminence in various fields and for fame and success, yet I feel safe in saying that it is the one city above all others from which young women should stay away," continued Dr. Young. "Let me qualify that. It is the one city which they should not seek out unless they have exceptional talents and abilities, so that they can cope successfully with the tremendous competition which they will encounter, or unless they are well supplied with funds to tide them over their weeks or months of job-hunting, or to carry them back to their homes if they face ultimate disappointment.

"New York is friendly to the young adventurer who comes provided with money for emergencies, but she turns a cold shoulder to the one who lacks foresight and goes broke in her midst.

"An unbelievably large number of girls drift into New York daily with only a few dollars in their purses, buoyed up by high hopes and ill-founded optimism. Back home they have painted an illusory picture of New York life and they are terrifically confident about their own capabilities. Many of them believe that they are destined to be great writers, actresses, singers, artists, but after a few days of canvassing the agencies, the editorial offices or the studios they find that the city is surfeited with talent. Their funds become exhausted, their clothes shabby and sometimes their pride prevents them from letting the folks back home know their predicament. They wind up on park benches and, if their will power is poor, meet a deplorable and cruel fate.

"Many of these girls are compelled to come to the city because they cannot find employment on the farm or in the small town, especially when they must help contribute to the support of the family.

"Hence, they come to New York. I will tell you what happens to some of them here. Only the other day a young girl from Iowa sought out Mrs. Booth for help in her desperate situation. For nine days and nights she had walked the streets and slept on park benches, and in all that time she had eaten only about 20 ounces of food. She came to New York with $32. At home she had left a brother and sister, both afflicted with tuberculosis and a mother suffering from rheumatism. She had been in the habit of working very hard back in Iowa, even harvesting the grain with her brother. There was a small mortgage on their home, and it was the girl's intention to make enough money in New York to support the family at home and ease their sufferings. She was a pretty girl and fairly well dressed. She told Mrs. Booth that she had had offers of three different jobs, but to each one a detestable condition was attached.

"Never before have I heard a more shameful story—one reflecting on the decency and humanity of man. That girl's feet were bleeding. She had walked the streets for days seeking jobs without strings attached to them. Soon her money gave out and she was reduced to sleeping in parks. Finally, exhausted from lack of food and proper rest and filled with anxiety, she came to Mrs. Booth with her troubles. She was sent to our shelter on Twenty-third street, and first of all was fed, though the amounts of food given her had to be small at first because of her starved condition. A decent job was obtained for her and she remained at the shelter until she got her first week's salary. Then a decent room was found for her.

"Not long ago a welfare officer from the Seventh precinct here brought a young girl to our shelter. She had arrived at the police station, frantic and weeping, to sob out her sorry story at the desk. She came to New York from Rome, Ga., where she had left her mother, a very poor woman who was not in good health. The daughter had come to New York in the hope of obtaining a good-paying job so that she could provide medical attention for her mother. She found a job which paid her $15 a week, and out of this she had been sending her mother $7 a week. As a result of living on $8 a week, the girl's own health was broken, her clothes were shabby and she confessed that she had been forced to pawn her mother's wedding ring, which had been given to her as a parting gift when she left Georgia.

"Sobbing this girl held forth a telegram she had just received. The police lieutenant read it. The message told her that her mother was dying. The welfare officer brought her to our shelter and we immediately gave her the railroad fare to Rome, enough money to buy food on the way and $30 in addition. We learned later that she had arrived just in time, for her mother died shortly after she got there. That girl had learned a bitter lesson in New York. She had lived there just nine weeks and had encountered nothing but deprivation, though she had secured a job. After her mother's death she decided that she must abandon her dreams of a great future, for she had originally come to New York not only to help take care of her sick mother but also to make a place for herself in the world of the theater. She thought she had great talent and was merely holding down her $15-a-week job until some manager should discover her and give her her great chance.

"She is now working in a drug store back in Rome and is earning $18 a week, which provides for her fairly well in a town where living expenses are not nearly so high as in New York. Very sensibly she has come to a realization that, after all, she is a very ordinary girl with no outstanding talent whatsoever. She sent us $10, a sum which she wanted us to use to help some other poor girl as badly off as she had been and which was her way of showing appreciation for the help we had given her.

"OUR Philadelphia branch one day received a letter from a father in Virginia telling us about his young daughter, who, after her mother's death, had run away from home, with Philadelphia as her destination. He had never heard from her again. He sent us her photograph and we had copies made of it, which we gave to our slum workers. Some time afterward one of our missionaries, on her rounds of investigation, chanced to visit a notorious place. On the second floor she found a girl lying on a bed of rags in a pitiable condition. She was ill and delirious, an opium smoker. Our organization immediately removed her from the dive. She was too ill to talk. When she had recovered somewhat we learned her story. She proved to be the girl from West Virginia, whose father was hunting for her, at the time. While this was a case which reached us a little late, for we deal mostly in preventive measures, we nevertheless decided to help this girl. We sent her to a fresh-air farm in Pennsylvania, where she was cared for 16 weeks and eventually nursed back to health. Upon her recovery there was a reunion with her family and she is now happily engaged in social work.

"While many of these young girls who come to New York each year use poor judgment and are the victims of self-deception, believing that mediocrity is talent, all of them do not fall into this classification. Some of these girls who become stranded are not spinning golden fantasies in which they figure as Broadway stars, motion picture queens, famous artists or writers. They come to New York from the farms and the small towns of the country because they must work and there is nothing suitable there for them to do. They are willing to work at anything, as maids or waitresses, but even these humbler occupations are not always to be found.

"But even though this situation exists, the modern girl is better able to emerge from her predicament than the girl of another day. Years ago girls would have hesitated to leave home in the first place, feeling that they were unequipped to fight the battle of life in a big city alone and unprotected. Today their independence and self-confidence bring them to New York in hordes. And it is the modern, more or less unconventional attitude of young girls, criticized by the older generation, which helps them in their hour of distress. Years ago a girl would have had too much so-called pride to appeal to her people or to philanthropic organizations for assistance, stumbling as a result into pitfalls left open for the penniless girl in a big city, but today she doesn't care so much what people think. Rather than compromise herself or run the risk of falling in with disreputable people who might offer her temporary aid, she bravely and wisely approaches the police or relief organizations and frankly reveals her plight. It is a vastly safer method than the old one of pride and concealment.

"With the condition of women so vastly changed, more and more girls are assuming more difficult tasks and greater responsibilities toward their families. Due to the increased liberties for girls and their changed status in the economic and social world, large numbers of them are being magnetized in the direction of the big cities.

"MANY thousands of young women coming to New York, with the best of intentions and for compelling reasons, become stranded and hopelessly discouraged. At such a time these girls need all the elementary necessities of life. They need counsel, friendship and help, which will give them a fresh start before they sink into a state of despair and loneliness. The first of these necessities is a place to live. It is both strange and pathetic that in spite of New York City's great philanthropic and well organized relief agencies, there are practically no homes of this character for the self-respecting girl. There are well conducted hotels or homes for girls who are earning fairly good wages. In all these institutions the charge, however reasonable, is prohibitive for the girl who has nothing or at best only a few dollars left. There are numerous homes for so called 'fallen women'; but for the self-respecting girl who is stranded in our city and faces disaster far from home and unknown to loved ones, practically no provision is made.

"The Volunteers of America are planning to erect and maintain in the heart of New York a building in which shelter and help will be given to such women and girls. In addition to housing accommodations, there will be provided an adequate social life, educational facilities, opportunity for economic betterment, a simple religious culture and a home atmosphere. The purpose is prevention, not redemption; to forestall disgrace and disaster, not to rescue and reclaim. The institution is to be a temporary shelter. During the stay of the woman or girl efforts will be made either for her return home, when that seems desirable, or for her economic and social placement and improvement. No charge will be made either for room or board if the girl is unable to pay. When she has found employment, payment will be accepted in proportion to her earnings; when she has found sufficiently remunerative work, a good permanent home or boarding house will be found for her and she will make room for the girl who has nothing."

Document 51. Newspaper page, the Omaha *World Herald*, November 24, 1929. [National Archives]

Document 52. Photograph, "still," n.d. [National Archives]

reach a verdict.

A Sign and a Shot

Border patrolmen have been trying to halt the smuggling of liquor from Canada into Minnesota. It is a regulation, that when they set up a sign along a road, cars driving past must halt to be searched. Last Saturday a car containing a man, his wife and two children drove past such a sign near International Falls. According to the wife—who became a widow immediately afterward—they were driving slowly and were not yet entirely past the sign when a fusillade of bullets swept the car. The bullets were fired without warning and one of them struck the husband in the back of the neck, killing him instantly. An examination of the car showed no contraband. "I only did my duty," said the border patrol who fired into a family party.

Had he suspected the driver of being merely a bank robber, or perhaps a fugitive murderer, we doubt if he would have raked with his shotgun a car in which obviously there were innocent persons riding. But because he suspected that a quart or perhaps a gallon or two, of liquor was passing, he "shot to kill" to quote a customs order alleged to have been issued from Duluth. This was just one of those things that happen under prohibition.

A Province of the Hills

City Council of Baltimore
City Hall

Baltimore, January 24, 1922.

Mr. Hon. Calvin Coolidge,
President of the United States Senate,
Washington, D. C.

We hereby certify that the following Resolution was adopted in both Branches of the City Council of Baltimore on the dates as specified: First Branch January 16, 1922; Second Branch January 23, 1922:-

RESOLUTION RELATING TO THE VOLSTEAD ACT.

Whereas, the enactment and passage of the Federal Prohibition Act has failed to meet with the approval of the general public throughout the country; and

Whereas, while most comprehensive, drastic and summary in its character and scope, efforts to enforce same at vast public expense, have utterly failed to obtain and secure for it due and proper respect and obedience on the part of the people; and

Whereas, abundant statistics of unimpeachable nature fully and conclusively demonstrate the fact that the general public is opposed to existing prohibition laws which deprive people in the natural and customary use and consumption of stimulating beverages; and

Whereas, a general survey of conditions throughout the country suggests a reasonable and liberal modification of prohibition laws which will permit the manufacture, sale and distribution of wholesome beers and light wines; therefore

Be it resolved by both Branches of the City Council of Baltimore, that the Congress of the United States of America be and it is hereby respectfully requested to amend and modify the existing Prohibition Law, known as the Volstead Act, in order to permit the manufacture, sale and distribution of wholesome beers and light wines, and that all governmental revenue derived from such permission be set aside and used as a separate fund for the payment of bonuses to ex-service men; and be it further

Resolved, that the General Assembly of Maryland be and it is hereby requested to petition the Congress of the United States to amend and modify the Volstead Act as above set forth; and be it further

Resolved, that the Chief Clerk of the First Branch City Council be and he is hereby directed to send a copy of this resolution to the President of the U. S. Senate, the Speaker of the House of Representatives of the U. S., the President of the Maryland State Senate and the Speaker of the House of Delegates.

Very respectfully,

Gilbert A. Dailey
Chief Clerk First Branch City Council.

Chief Clerk Second Branch City Council.

Document 54. Resolution to the Hon. Calvin Coolidge from the City Council of Baltimore, January 24, 1922. [National Archives]

THE NAME "CHISCA" ORIGINATED IN THE NAME OF AN INDIAN CHIEF
AND OF HIS VILLAGE ON THE CHICKASAW BLUFFS
WHERE NOW STANDS MEMPHIS

Hotel Chisca

RECEIVED
JUL 1 9 1929

NATIONAL COMMISSION ON LAW
OBSERVANCE AND ENFORCEMENT

MEMPHIS, TENN.   July 17 '29

PIOMINGO
CHICKASAW CHIEFTAIN -
from an authentic sketch from Life

Prohibition

Mr.G.W.Wickersham,
Washington,D.C.
        Dear Sir;

        Have just read that you say that
"Justice to be effective should be speedy".

 A very true saying;but a better one would be
this; "Justice to be effective should be impartial."

        The law will take up a negro or
poor white man who has one-half pint in his house
and wink at the wealthy man who has 2oo gallons in
his house.   A rich man here,crated up 25 cases
of good whiskey,a few days ago and shipped it to
Kansas City.   He had kept it in his residence
for many years and neither State or Federal law
dared touch it,neither did either authority take
notice,the other day,when he moved it.

        There is plenty of law in regard to
curbing or controling large combinations of money
in the United States. These laws are being violat-
ed every day; Will your Commission take notice of
this?   Am enclosing some clippings--Read
and see what the Writers think of your Commission.

        One clipping tells of Capt.Lee,a
Memphis Millionare who was caught red handed with
i75 gallons of Liquor on his Wharf,but being this
rich,neither the State Grand Jury or the Federal
Authorities,care to bother Mr.Lee.

        Had he been a Negro or poor white,he
would be looking thru the bars at this time.
                        Yours very truly
                        Citizen of Arkansas.

WASHINGTON COUNTY

WOMEN'S CHRISTIAN TEMPERANCE UNION

Claysville, Pa., Jan. 6, 1926.

Hon. Frank B. Kellogg,
    Sec. of State, Washington, D. C.

My dear Sir:

We note the fact that the International Society for the liberty to make Alcohol in every country is planning to meet in our national capital on Jan. 16th. We believe this to be a movement of brewers, distillers, and wine growers, many of them foreigners, in a fight against the American constitution.

Such a meeting, we believe should be prevented under the authority of the Federal Government. If undesirable persons can be expelled, why not prohibit the entrance of those who are coming to attack the constitution of the United States?

As a representative of more than seven hundred active members of W. C. T. U. and more than three hundred honorary members of the same organization, I most sincerely solicit your attention to this matter.

Very respectfully yours,

Mrs. W. C. Hair

County president of Women's Christian Temperance Union of Washington County, Pa.

Document 56. Letter to the Hon. Frank B. Kellogg from Mrs. W. C. Hair, January 6, 1926. [National Archives]

Miss Mabel Willebrant,
Ass't. Attorney General for
Prohibition,
Washington, D. C.

Dear Madame:-

      Prohibition has been enforced for nine
years, but it has never been enforced in a proper way as
everyone knows especially in this section of the country.

      I have reported several times to the
Prohibition unit in New Jersey as well as to the Police Dept.
in Newark, N. J. of the exsistence of two places which ought
to be entirely closed and padlocked, and the owners sent
back where they belong as they are not even citizens of the
United States.

      The first place is at the corner of
Wood Street and Seventh Avenue in the City of Newark. By whom
it is held no one knows, but the real fact is that the
liquor is manufactured and sold right in the place under the
eyes of boys and girls of young age, and it is across the
street from the Second Precint Police Station. If the place
is protected by the Police, no one knows, and why the Prohibition unit for New Jersey has done nothing is also a mistake.

      The second place is ran as a Grill Room
at 174 Bloomfield Avenue by a notorious bootlegger by the
name of Carmine Sica. This place is frequented by City
Officials, and anyone that may pass in front of that door on
Saturday evenings has a disgusting pleasure to see girls below
eighteen to come down semi-nude and drunk, and go in taxi cabs
with men, etc.

      Kindly see if you can do anything to
suppress these two places, and also your personality is not
known to anyone still you deserve a lot of credit for your
activity in the premises.

               Very truly yours,

               O. A. Calandria

      P. S. If anything would be done, please do not
do it through New York Operators as they know the New Jersey
people very well.

Document 57. Letter to Miss Mabel[sic] Willebran[d]t
from O. A. Calandria, n.d. [National Archives]

United States Spends Millions Of Dollars To Ban Liquor But Teaches Thousands Just How To Make It

BY RODNEY DUTCHER

Washington—Certain congressmen have worked themselves into a lather of moral indignation because the government had operated a speakeasy to trap bootleggers.

But you ain't heard nothin' yet!

The government for some time has been engaged in sending recipes and formulae to its citizens telling them how to make alcoholic beverages which the law forbids one to manufacture. It is teaching them by the tens, if not by the hundreds, of thousands.

JUST WRITE AND ASK

That is, while one branch of the government tries to enforce prohibition laws and puts horrid stuff into all the alcohol, two other branches are instructing householders in the most approved methods of making real pre-war stuff. These two branches are Congress, which receives requests for formulae, and the government printing office, which publishes all government documents and congressional speeches and cheerfully furnishes whatever is wanted.

Would you make your own rye or bourbon whisky? Write to your congressman.

Would you like a few casks of Port, Claret or Burgundy in the cellar? Your congressman will be pleased to tell you how.

Would you experiment with lowly home brew? This formula, too, awaits your call.

HOME BREW

Here's how the system works:

A letter recently came to a dry congressman from a constituent. It said: "Please tell me how to make home brew."

Constituents must be pleased. This congressman's conscientious secretary found the Department of Agriculture's Year Book for 1904. Pages 370-378 furnished complete processes for manufacture of all sorts of wines, from ordinary wines to angelicas and a couple of brandies.

Then she heard about Jan. 3 speech of Congressman E. Hull of Peoria, Ill., on the medicinal spirits bill. Hull formerly headed a big distillery in Peoria and is regarded sometimes as this country's foremost authority on hard liquor. He had explained at length the process of making three grades of spirits, including rye, bourbon, malt, gin, brandies and others. This speech went into the Congressional Record and also is available in pamphlet form.

The congressman's secretary was not aware that the government could furnish a recipe for beer, but it can and does, thanks to Congressman Emanuel Celler of New York, who last year introduced into the Record George Washington's famous recipe for beer.

Thus, here are three publications with which any bootlegger can set up stock. There has been a big rush for all three.

GETS 10,000 REQUESTS

Congressman Hull's office has filled more than 10,000 requests for copies of his speech.

Congressman Celler's office has not kept track, but there was a big rush for the beer recipe in the months following the speech and the demand continues fairly brisk. There is still a good supply of both the Hull and Celler speeches and the government printing office is always ready to print more when asked.

Perhaps all this interest is merely academic. But it is a more than interesting situation which finds the taxpayers contributing many millions annually to keep the nation dry and simultaneously paying printing and mailing costs for the dissemination of recipes for whiskey, wine, beer and hard cider.

Fo

Mr. Henry C. Wallace,
Wash., D. C.

Dear Mr. Secretary:

 Railroad strike that you've heard about. Street car strike in Chicago. One million gallons of gasoline more a day. Coal strike. More coal oil is all. Ten million automobiles, tractors, airplanes. Run the price of oils up and the price of horse feed down. Billions of dollars for the Standard Oil Co. Let them run the Government.

 Now Mr. Secretary if not asking to much will you please tell a poor farmer that owns 480 acres of land why the Government will not allow the manufacture of pure grain alchol to run some of these engines with? Or will we have to wait until the Standard Oil gets hold of all the chemical plants? You are aware that they can run an automobile just as far and cheap on a gallon of pure grain alchol as they can on gasoline I suppose. I can show you. I do not want it to drink as I never took a drink in my life but I have talked to the farmers all over fourteen states and they are all going broke. What do you expect us to do?

      Yours truly,

       (Signed) J. O. Robertson,

        Beardstown, Ill.

Aug. 14.

Document 59. Letter to Mr. Henry C. Wallace from
J. O. Robertson, August 14, 1922. [National Archives]

Document 60. Cartoon, Columbus *Dispatch,* January 21, 1931. [National Archives]

National Cigarette Law Enforcement League Inc.

EXECUTIVE COMMITTEE

Dr. Dean C. Dutton, Pres.
Norman, Okla.
Dr. Wm. Forney Hovis, 1st Vice-Pres.
Oklahoma City, Okla.
Prof. J. R. Barton, 2rd Vice-Pres.
Oklahoma City, Okla.
Judge Jas. I. Phelps, 3rd Vice-Pres.
Oklahoma City, Okla.
Prof. Earl P. Weston, 4th Vice Pres.
Comanche, Okla.
Rev. Alva P. Jones, Supt.
Oklahoma City, Okla.
Mr. L. A. Coppage, Treas.
Oklahoma City, Okla.
Mr. D. N. Downing, Secy.
Oklahoma City, Okla.
Prof. Festus C. Snow, Auditor
Comanche, Okla.
Gov. Wm. J. Holloway, Council.
Hugo, Okla.

125 W. 17th St.   Phone 4 - 9226

Other Director

Dr. Fred Mesch
Stillwater, Okla.
Mr. Ed L. Klein
Oklahoma City, Okla.
Cong. Jed Johnson
Anadarko, Okla.
Rev. L. H. La Grone
Blackwell, Okla.
Prof. C. W. Gethman
Oklahoma City, Okla.
Mrs. Alice M. David
Oklahoma, Okla.
Prof. Jno. S. Voughn
Durant, Okla.
Mr. U. M. Baughman
Oklahoma City, Okla.
Mr. Jno. A. Simpson
Oklahoma City, Okla.
Mr. Jno. W. Heidbrink
Oklahoma City, Okla.

Oklahoma City, Okla., **May. 25,** ....19..**29**

To The Honorable Herbert Hoover, President,
United States of America,
Washington, D. C.

Dear Mr. President:

I understand that while you were Secretary of the Interior you gave out a statement saying, "There is no agency in the world today that is so seriously affecting the health, education, efficiency and character of boys and girls as the cigarette habit. Nearly every delinquent is a cigarette smoker."

Dr. C. L. Barber, former President of the Medico-Physical Research Association of America said, "This great wave of crime is due to the use of cigarettes and nothing else. The indiscriminate use of hooch, poison liquor, wine, Jamaica ginger and any other product that has a kick, is due to the use of cigarettes and nothing else." That, "You may legislate all the Volstead Acts, or any other acts you have a mind to, but you never will stop this wave of crime and demoralization until you stop the manufacture and sale of cigarettes."

Concerning "Acrolein," one of the 20 different poisons in the smoke of a cigarette, Mr. Edison says, "Ireally believe acrolein often makes boys insane." And Dr. Forbes Winslow says, "Cigarette smoking is one of the chief causes of insanity."

In view of these and like statements, from other eminent authorities, would it not be a fine idea for your crime commission of eminent jurists to make a careful study of the bearing of cigarette smoking upon the criminal? And especially Mr. Hoover, since there are forty states of our Union which are trying to protect their future citizens from the cigarette evil by passing laws prohibiting the sale of cigarettes and cigarette papers to their youths?

If cigarette smoking helps to produce criminals, it may be necessary to prohibit this evil before our crime wave can be ultimately solved (?)

With great faith in the success of your administration, I am,

Most cordially,

Alva P. Jones.

Superintendent,
National Cigarette Law Enforcement League.

APJ/MS.

Document 61. Letter to the Hon. Herbert Hoover, President, from Alva P. Jones, May 25, 1929. [National Archives]

1309 Franklin St.,

Johnstown, Pa.,

Sept. 10, 1929.

The National Law Enforcement Commission,

Washington, D. C.

Gentlemen:

I understand that a committee has been appointed to study the cause of crime. This is very important indeed. For their consideration I beg to present a few things:

1. I enclose the front cover page of one copy of "Short Stories". I consider such pictures in our magazines and such stories which constantly tell of shooting *and other crimes* as a most prolific source of crime, for the young folks who see them and read them are inspired to do the same.

2. Moving Pictures *are* another source of crime. This has been proven again and again. For in many moving pictures crime is displayed and often the hero is guilty of crime himself, and so children are led to believe it is smart to commit a crime and often the proper thing to do.

These are two main causes of crime which could be largely eliminated by the following legislation:

All pictures of crime are prohibited on the screen, advertising posters, magazines and newspapers, etc.

All stories told so as to condone crime or praise it should be positively forbidden.

3. The ease with which people in America can buy firearms and ammunition is the greatest cause of crime in America. Why should every one indiscriminately be allowed to have a weapon?

I have lived for 25 years in India and with that large population we do not have as many crimes in a year as some of our cities

have in a month. Why is it? Because/ the sale of firearms is restricted.
No one can buy a weapon or ammunition without a license from the Government, neither can he sell it to some one else . In this way the Gov.
knows exactly how many people have firearms and who they are. Every year
a check is made of all of them. If any one is found guilty of misusing
his privilege to own a weapon his license is revoked and the weapon is
taken from him. Only decent and trustworthy people can secure a license,
and then only if they can show sufficient reason why they should have
the permission.

Until the U.S. passes some law similar to this we cannot
hope to reduce crime in America materially. Most crimes are committed
by shooting, and the most wicked criminal can always secure a weapon.
There is no constraint.

I recommend tp you these three causes for your consideration, and trust you may urge legislation to curb these evils.

Very sincerely yours,

J. M. Blough.

A Novel of Railroad Gunmen by Chas. W. Tyler

ShortStories

Twice A Month

30c in Canad.

JULY 10th   **25¢**

WILLIAM MACLEOD RAINE'S

NEW NOVEL BEGINS WITH HUMMING LEAD!

The Fighting Tenderfoot

Looks for Trouble

LAW OFFICES
OF

GEARY & RANKIN

CHESTER, PA.

June 6, 1929.

Hon. George W. Wickersham,
Law Enforcement Commission,
Washington, D. C.

Dear Mr. Wickersham:

To begin with, I am convinced that you told the truth in your address yesterday.

For some time, I have been inclined to believe that our compulsory education laws, as they exist, contribute somewhat to the criminal class. In this State, a youth, until sixteen years of age, is prohibited from working and compelled to attend school. There are a large number of boys not bent toward a school education, and in addition to avoiding study, we find them loitering around street corners, pool rooms, etc., with the result that when they arrive at sixteen years of age, they have not been trained to work, and it is practically impossible to persuade them to work. From that class, come many of our hold-up men, gunmen, etc.

You have probably noted that the greater part of the criminal class is made up of young men.

Very truly,

A. B. Geary

ABG:ALH

Document 63. Letter to the Hon. George W. Wickersham from A. B. Geary, June 6, 1929. [National Archives]

GEORGE W. DEXTER
ATTORNEY AT LAW
MARYLAND CASUALTY BUILDING
BALTIMORE

June 10, 1929

Hon. Geo. W. Wickersham
Chairman Law Enforcement Committee
Department of Justice
Washington, D. C.

Sir:

I trust that you will pardon this unsolicited observation, but I believe I voice the sentiments of good citizens everywhere in saying that there is more interest perhaps than you are aware in the result of the deliberations of the splendid committee of which you are the chairman.

First, it seems that justice is defeated in some instances by virtue of information given out for publication by police officers and prosecuting attorneys in advance of the capture of those charged with crime and prior to the time that they are actually tried. Doubtless the desire to appear in the public press is the cause in both instances, but the result is the same as the criminals can follow the daily developments through the newspapers and make their escape if not yet captured, or prepare their defense if not yet tried.

Second, the newspapers seem to be making law enforcement more difficult by giving crime great value as "news" and assigning headlines accordingly. It is also treating the capture and conviction of many accused of crime as something of a sporting event. The press is not urging law enforcement as it might do. On the contrary, by editorials and by cartoons, it sometimes actually ridicules acts of public officials engaged in capture and prosecution of those charged with crime and holds public officials and others interested up to ridicule. There are few men who can withstand ridicule. It is the most subtle of instruments thus employed, and particularly when used as cartoons. Indeed it seems, to some at least, that the misguided value of crime as news and the misdirected attitude of the newspapers at the present time would constitute the greatest single deterrent to law enforcement.

I am sure that your committee will consider this feature along with all the others, but you will pardon me in saying that possibly a changed attitude on the part of newspapers would go further than any other agency in bringing about the end your committee so much desires.

Very respectfully,

Geo W Dexter

GWD:AER

Document 64. Letter to the Hon. George W. Wickersham from
George W. Dexter, June 10, 1929. [National Archives]

108 Laurent St.
Santa Cruz. Calif.
June 16. 1929.

Mr. Geo. W. Wickersham.
Chairman Law Enforcement Commission,
Washington. D.C.

Dear Sir:

The neglect of apprenticeship in America has a great deal to do with unemployment and this in turn leads to lawbreaking.

Thousands of those in our reformatories are there because they never had a chance to lear a trade.

Many of them wasted their precious time in public school tinkering with a cut-down fliver instead of preparing for a trade.

Automotive work was introduced into our schools as a war measure. This was a sad mistake.

The sooner it is taken out the better.

Inclosed documents have been sent to President Hoover, the Secretary of the Interior, the Secretary of Labor and the Commissioner of Education.

Trusting this material will be of some use to the Commission.

I am,

very truly yours,

Wm. T. Elzinga.

Hollywood, California, August 5, 1929.

My Dear Mr. President.-

Ihave been particularly interested in press
notices regarding your commission for the study of crime. As a
newspaper man of about twenty-five years standing and through my
experiences as a big brother etc.,I have come in contact with many
criminals,especially among the younger generation and I have discovered that a majority of the boys who become criminals have
been more or less forced into such a life through lack of employment,attempting to hold down jobs which they were unfitted for and
disliked or because they were the product of broken homes.

Personally I believe if the unemployment situation
was cleaned up crime would decrease very perceptibly. Of course it
may be conceit or ego but I believe that I have a solution for the
unemployment situation. That is the reason for this letter.

Idle men and women are like idle machines,a lia-
bility instead of an asset. Unlike machines,idle humans must eat
and sleep and,if they can not secure employment,than many of them
take other methods of procuring these things. Usually criminal
methods.

Now supposing every merchant,every manufacturer
and other employers of labor were to put on every man or woman they
could what would happen? For a time they would be an expense but
does it not stand to reason that when all of these additional persons were working and earning money that it would stimulate buying? And would not all of the companies xxx benefit through this

employment? Think of the additional money that would be put into circulation. Idle men and women do not spend money but men and women who are employed do. It seems to me that if a movement such as I suggest was launched the unemployment situation would be materially helped and business would show a decided improvement.

I may be way off but at any rate I thought it would not do any harm to lay this idea before your commission. Some good might come of it and that is all I want.

Having been a Washington correspondent some years age I realize full well that this letter stands no chance of falling into your hands but it might by luck be submitted to the commission.

Very truly

Arthur R. Boyden
R.K.O. Studios
Hollywood, Calif.

New England Club
OF SEATTLE

CRIME, and LAW ENFORCEMENT

Ever since President Hoover gave his stinging indictment of the lawlessness and lack of character shown by the American people since the War, an extensive agitation of conscience is being shown, and a serious intention to study the causes and remedies for thesame.

It is being widely charged that much the greater part of the vicious forms of crime are committed by recent immigrants who have not yet learned the necessity for conforming to the statutes and restrictions of our government, and especially those who are subject to certain alien political church influences. Even if true, this does not relieve our American citizens from any of the responsibility. We invited them, and encouraged them-until recently-to come here and help build up the country. In return for which, we undertook to civilize them and make them equal as citizens. Now that we have failed to do so, it is our fault; and we shalll continue to be severely punished as at present until we meet the responsibility.

The first thing to be observed, perhaps, is that the increase of crime is not from the increase of netural criminals, but the great increase of criminal opportunity afforded by the invention of the auto. The easy means by which the auto can be used for robbery of all sorts, kidnapping and murder, as well as the disposing of liquor, have caused a vast increase in those forms of crime. And in close connection with these lie all of the evils of the liquor traffic and drinking. For the liquor evils, sporting business and professional men, fashionable society and a certain type of newspapers

Document 67a. Letter to Crime and Law Enforcement [Commission]
from John E. Ayer, M. V., May 23, 1929. [National Archives]

are almost wholly responsible. Without the present liquor laws, the conditions would certainly be vastly worse than at present. The great mass of the people, the farmers, mechanics and the labor ranks are far nore sober and law abiding than they were before the Prohibition Amendment; and as those classeswil furnish practically all of the parentage of the future, their interest is the only one entitled to consideration.

The checking of the crime wave is not merely a moral, or good citizenship issue. It is quite as much a matter of self preservation. The ominous increase of the deadly forces of electricity and gasoline in all industries and locomotion, and the well known fact that any drinking of alcohol affects the sight, caution and judgment in the brain, has made it imperative that all liquor drinking must be suppressed; no matter how much it may conflict with self indulgence or 'personal liberty'. It cannot be dodged by any such absurd farce as a certain portion of the Press is now exhibiting with its mass of letters. There is no line of practicable compromise. A beer and wine compromise would demoralize the whole country and negative all enforcement. It cannot be shirked by loading the responsibility on public officials. They can go but little further than juries will back them with unanimous votes. There must be a strong general backing of the efforts of the President,-the first President who has ever shown a positive purpose and ability to deal with the worst evils of society-by the daily volunteer propaganda work of all decent citizens.

John E. AYER, M. V.

420 Haight Bldg. Seattle, Wn

May 23-29

The Shreveport Times

THE TIMES PUBLISHING COMPANY, LTD.

Robert Ewing...President and Publisher
John D. Ewing..Associate Publisher
L. A. Mailhes..Business Manager
Albert Witt..Managing Editor

MEMBERS OF THE ASSOCIATED PRESS

The Associated Press is exclusively entitled to the use for publication of all news dispatches credited to it or not otherwise credited to the paper and also the local news published herein

REPRESENTATIVES—John M. Braham Company, London Guarantee and Accident Building, Chicago; Graybor Building, New York; Chemical Building, St. Louis; Kresge Building, Detroit; 501 Montgomery Street, San Francisco; Land and Bank Building, Kansas City; Candler Building, Atlanta; Chamber of Commerce Building, Los Angeles, California; Leary Building, Seattle, Washington.

SUBSCRIPTION RATES

Daily and Sunday	Daily Only by Mail	Sunday Only by Mail
12 Months $7.50	12 Months $5.00	12 Months $2.60
6 Months 4.00	6 Months 2.50	6 Months 1.30
3 Months 2.15	3 Months 1.50	3 Months ...... .75
1 Month .... .75	1 Month ...... .50	1 Month ...... .25

Payable in Advance

A DISTINGUISHED PRISONER.

It is fitting, we suppose, that a character of Al Capone's eminent standing in the crime world should not be harassed with ordinary prison rules and conventions during his stay in the Holmesburg jail. Philadelphia prison authorities seldom have an opportunity to entertain so distinguished a gunman and "pineapple" distributor as the gentleman from Chicago to whom the euphonious title of "Scarface" has been given in the police records. So it is proper that they should vie with each other in their efforts to make the prison stay of their Chicago guest pleasant.

At any rate, they are doing it. Other Holmesburg prisoners are limited in their contact with the outside world to two censored letters per month. Not so Al. He has been permitted to hold long distance telephone conversations and send telegrams ad lib.

Ninety-nine per cent of the prison population eats jail fare. "Scarface" is permitted to treat himself to toothsome delicacies. He does not sleep on a prison cot, but in a downy bed as soft and comfortable as that in any first-class hotel. Prison guards fight each other for the privilege of running errands for him. Except in the single particular that he has not his freedom, Al is not a prisoner but a public guest. And just now, "Scarface" needs the security of bolts and bars!

We have frequently heard that there is a law for the poor and a law for the rich, and eminent criminologists have scoffed at it. But the aphorism is true, just the same. Money is as potent an influence behind prison walls as outside of them. When Al Capone was arrested, he had $10,000 in his possession. It will be interesting to know how much of this sum is left when the prison doors again open for him.

He has been treated like an honored guest and permitted to endure no hardships in jail. And, yet, Al Capone has amassed millions as a leader of organized criminals. There is hardly a crime on the police blotter that he has not committed many times. He has had men murdered as ruthlessly as he would remove worthless alley cats. He has suborned witnesses, bought protection from dishonest law officers, corrupted politicians and ~~threatened weak judges to such~~ an extent that his immunity from arrest was almost an American watchword. Impudently defying all law and authority, as cold-blooded and callous a wretch as ever escaped the hangman's noose, he is treated in prison like a king, losing only his liberty—which just now is of little value to him.

If, however, we are disposed to severely criticize the Philadelphia authorities for their treatment of Al Capone, let us reflect that we are not ourselves immune from some of the influences brought to bear in behalf of this racketeer and czar of the underworld. In many of our penitentiary trusties we find men of influence. Theirs is not the hard lot of the average convict. Their punishment is not nearly so severe as judge and jury intended it to be.

Favors in prison are not rare in any American state. They are only rare in countries where all men are equal before the law. And America is not one of them.

Document 68. Editorial, *The Shreveport Times*, May 5, 1929. [National Archives]

The Cleveland Press

(A SCRIPPS-HOWARD NEWSPAPER)

TED O. THACKREY, Editor—J. G. MEILINK, Business Manager
LOUIS B. SELTZER..........................Associate Editor
EDWARD T. AUSTIN.....................Managing Editor
ROBERT F. PAINE........Editor Emeritus

Full Reports of United Press, NEA Service and Scripps-Howard. Newspaper Alliance

Entered at Cleveland, Ohio, as second class mail matter. By mail in the First and Second Postal zones where there is no PRESS carrier, $3.00 per year. $6.00 a year elsewhere.

"Give Light and the People Will Find Their Own Way."—Daniel

NOT RECORDED

Is Justice Blind?

A MAN steals a watch and gets 10 years in the pen. Unlike Harry F. Sinclair, the oil multimillionaire, he cannot pull and twist a long delay from the law.

He goes to the pen—pronto!

When he, the man who steals the watch, gets there he is shown few, if any, favors. He goes to work in the prison shop. He gets a small cell as his home for 10 years, less time for good behavior.

Josiah Kirby was a "financial wizard." He got seven and a half years in Atlanta Penitentiary. The charges, using the mails to defraud, grew from his conduct of the $30,000,000 Discount Co., which collapsed, causing hundreds of small investors to lose their savings.

Kirby went to Atlanta in July, 1926. His term can be reduced by good behavior to six years and eight months. Count on Kirby to be "good."

In yesterday's issues of The Press, on Page One, was a small story about Kirby. He is now chauffeur for Warden John W. Snook of the Atlanta Pen. The story said Kirby sees "considerable of Atlanta from behind the steering wheel" of the warden's car.

One man steals a watch.

Another helps wreck a $30,000,000 enterprise.

A third tries to steal oil reserves worth many millions from the people.

The man who steals the watch goes to prison—pronto!

The man who helped wreck a $30,000,000 enterprise sees considerable of the country-side outside prison from the wheel of an auto.

The man who tries to steal a nation's oil reserves finds legal loopholes to escape jail.

Justice is presumed to be blind—blind to a man's economic status when he appears before her.

Ask the man who stole the watch.

Ask the "financial wizard."

Ask the oil multimillionaire.

Ask them—

Is Justice blind?

NOT RECORDED

226016-1

Teaching With Documents Order Form

The 1920's
You may order copies of the following documents in their original size:

Document	Price	Qty.	Total
Document 51. *(17x22, b/w)* Newspaper page, the Omaha World Herald, November 24, 1929.	$24.00		
Document 58. *(11x17, b/w)* Newspaper article, Appleton Post-Crescent, n.d.	$14.00		
Add 5% MD Sales Tax (if applicable)			
Shipping & Handling (Ground Shipping: $10.00, Air Shipping: $22.00)			
Total			

Billing Address:

_____

_____

_____

_____

Shipping Address: (if different from Billing Address)

_____

_____

_____

_____

☐ Check Enclosed payable to Graphic Visions Associates

☐ VISA   ☐ Mastercard   ☐ American Express

_____/_____/_____/_____/   _____/_____/

Credit Card Number   Exp. Date   Authorized Signature

(_____)_____   (_____)_____

Telephone   Fax

Mail Order To: Graphic Visions
640 East Diamond Avenue, Ste. F
Gaithersburg, MD 20877